AF450313

VAMPIRIST

A Book About Real Vampires

Cecilia Fredriksson

MAKABER

For more information:
info@ceciliafredriksson.net
www.ceciliafredriksson.net

Cover design: Cecilia Fredriksson
Cover photo: macniak via Canva.com

ISBN-13: 978-91-7773-448-2
First edition: March 2018

I strongly advise against trying the methods of bloodletting and blood consumption presented in this book.

Foreword

Vampires, do they exist?

Regardless of your answer to this question, this book may provide interesting reading and hopefully deepen your knowledge of one of today's growing subcultures. Do you believe that real vampires burn in sunlight, have fangs and are dressed in gothic black clothes? Do they shy away from holy symbols or do they have eternal life? If so, this book will challenge your perception of vampires and their existence in our world.

This book is not about how the vampire has been portrayed in fiction through history, even though I sometimes refer to books and movies in the genre. This is also not a book about the supernatural vampire that has frightened humanity through the ages. The books theme is about alive and breathing humans who have made vampirism a part of their lifestyle. They call themselves real vampires.

I will guide you through various definitions of what a real vampire is, and how come they claim to be among us. This book will also bring up different vampiric activites, authentic violent crimes, diseases, research and religious communities.

This book is meant to fill a gap in our understanding of vampires in our times with its unique outside perspective. I do not make any claims on writing a comprehensive overview of the subject, and the book should be read, primarily, for entertainment. You will become acquainted with several people who define themselves as vampires. The validity of the claims, I leave up to you to decide.

To facilitate readability, I have chosen to use the term 'vampirist' when I refer to those who define themselves as vampires. The term 'vampire' is used when I speak of the vampires in fiction or mythology.

Cecilia Fredriksson

Contents

PART I

From myth to reality

Chapter 1

A Historical Review

'Throughout the whole vast shadowy world of ghosts and demons there is no figure so terrible, no figure so dreaded and abhorred, yet dight with such fearful fascination, as the vampire.'

(From the book *The Vampire his kith and kin* by Montague Summers)

TODAY'S PORTRAYAL of the vampire as human-like stem from late 1800's pop culture, but the vampire myth is much older than that. Todays depiction of zombies is more accurate to the original vampire.

What we associate with vampires has thereby been drastically altered through time and there also are major differences around the world.

Folklore and Mystique

It is difficult to specify precisely when the vampire became a part of folklore. According to some sources it can be traced back to around 600 BC, while other claim that the myth originates from the 1200's. However, it was not until the 1700's when a vampire panic spread across parts of Europe. From several villages came stories of how the dead rose from their graves only to attack friends and family. The vampire could also haunt their surviving family members mentally, by inflicting nightmares upon them.

A common theme for these unfortunate souls was that they had not received remission of their sins. It could, for example, be bastards, criminals or people who had committed suicide. The sinful lives of these people, the myth goes, resulted in their body being unable to rest and decay. The soul was instead possessed by a demon that took control of the body and would rise from the grave to go on hunts under the cover of night to harass the living. Sometimes is was believed that the vampire rose to avenge their fate, which resulted in them only attacking 'pure' souls, meaning those who would find peace after death. Other theories also involves incest, witchcraft among people with red hair, blue eyes and babies being born with teeth. These were thought to run a higher risk of becoming vampires after dying.

To expose the alleged vampires, their graves would be dug up. Bodies that had not decomposed, had blood around their mouths, growing hair and nails, were a sure sign of the person being undead. The vampire could also 'look alive' with reddish cheeks and open eyes.

A lack of reflection in a mirror was also a sign of vampirism. I one would come across one of these beings, it was said that blessed silver bullets would be effective. Also, holy symbols and garlic were used to ward against their presence.

A stake through the heart is probably the most well-known way to kill a vampire and suspicions were confirmed if the dead would scream when the stake was oushed through the heart. Another way to make sure the body would not rise again, was to decapitate the body. A practice described in some folklore was to first place a coin in the mouth of the deceased, before decapitation. Others placed the severed head between the legs, burned it, or boiled it in vinegar. The head could also be crushed. A more harmless practice was to bury the body with the face down and throw holy water on the coffin.

These methods of making sure that the bodies would not rise again have been confirmed through archeological finds. The Swedish newspaper *Dagens Nyheter* reported the 14th of October 2014 that a grave had been found in Bulgarie where the medieval body's heart had been pierced with an iron rod. According to the article there are hundreds of examples like this, only in Bulgaria. In Poland, several 'vampire graves', have been found. Heavy stones had been placed on the bodies, possibly to stop the dead from rising. In some cases, the stones had been placed over the throat and even the mouth. In other cases, the head had been removed and placed between the legs.

Most vampire myths are at least one hundred years old, but there are examples of modern myths of these nightwalkers. The Highgate cemetery in London has had a history of mysterious events happening that got much media attention in the 1970's. Two central figures in the birth of this modern myt hare David Farrant (author and occultist) and Seàn Manchester (author and exorcist). In December 1969, Farrans decided to spend the night at the Highgate cemetary. According to his statement, on this night he had a meeting with a grey being and decided to write a letter to the local newspaper *Hampstead and Highgate Express* to solicit the public for similar experiences. A number of stories from readers were sent in, all taking place in or around the cemetary, but all different from each other. The newspaper continued to report of the mysterious events that took place, and one day they published an interview with Seàn Manchester, who presented his theory of the happenings. His theory was remarkably specific. He said in the intervire that the events happening at Highgate cemetary were because of a Romanian magician of the black arts, whose coffin had been moved to England in the early 1900's. The so-called 'Vampire King' is said to have had several followers who bought him a house at West End. He was buried at the Highgate cemetary and Manchester further claimed that modern Satanists had 'awakened' the body back from the dead. Manchester suggested that the best solution would be to stick a stake through the heart, decapitate the body and burn it. During this time, both Farrant and Manchester reported on finding of dead foxes at the cemetary. The foxes were said to have wounds on their necks and were drenched in blood. The rivalry between Farrant and Manchester escalated, since they both wanted to be the one to expel or kill the vampire. As a response to the rivalry, Manchester arranged a vampire hunt at the cemetary, that would that place on the 13th of March 1970. This event, like the previous events, was also covered extensively by the media. Over one hundred people are said to have participated, but sadly, no vampire was caught. In 1985, Manchester published his book, *The Highgate Vampire*, in which he writes the stories of his excursions to the cemetary. On one of these trips, he said that he had broken into a catacomb where he found empty coffins that he filled with garlic, and then threw holy water on them. Manchester claims to a few years later, having found the body of a vampire, that he burned after driving a stake through it. The 1st of August 1970 the police found a decapitated body not far from the previously mentioned catacomb. The findings resulted in the police increasing their presence in the area. Shortly after the police had begun their surveillance, Farrant was arrested in the cemetary, armed with a crucifix and wooden stake, but the case was later shut down by the police. Four years later he would, however, be arrested and sentenced to jail for desecrating graves. He proclaimed innocense and claimed that Satanists were to blame. The myth about the Highgate vampire is to this day very much alive is focus of tourist attractions and guided tours.

Medical Explanations

Some who are believed to have become vampires, have likely suffered by unknown diseases. If the disease was hereditary, it could explain the belief that the vampire only attacked the most immediate family. In most cases, however, the bodies were just exacly that, bodies, and some rare cases of people being buried alive by mistake. Considering the flawed medical knowledge of the time in combination with superstition, it is understandable that people believed these to be cases of vampirism.

Today we know that bodies can make sudden movements shortly after death, but our forefathers believed that any movement post mortem was a mindful act of the deceased. They believed that any movement, color change or changes in size on the body were conscious actions. It is, for example, not uncommon for the nails to fall off the deceased, which may give the illusion of new nails having been formed.

Both nails and hair may become more prominent, and look longer, because the body is losing liquid post mortem. Gases in the body can also make the body look bloated, like they have just fed. Bodily fluids, such as blood, can start seeping out of the body through openings, like the mouth. Gases left in the body may also cause sounds. A body having its chest pierced by a stake may be 'screaming' as the gases and air is being forcefully pushed out. Bodies also, commonly, have a reddish hue, which may have given our forefathers the impressions that they had just fed.

A body can, quite frankly, look unnerving and even terrifying, though the causes are natural. There are, however, a number of diseases that have been linked with the myth of the vampire. A common illness linked with the vampire myth is anemia. Anemia comes from the Latin word anaemia. It is a condition in which you don't have enough red blood cells to carry adequate oxygen to the body's tissues. The condition may have several causes and goes under different names, depending on the cause of the anemia. When a patient suffers from anemia, the body may feel weak and the symptoms may be paleness, dizziness and lethargy. The most common cause for anemia is iron deficiency. Beyond the most common symptoms caused by iron deficiency, more uncommon symptoms includes damage to the mucous membranes, which is caused by the skin becoming more fragile. Iron supplement pills are often the go-to alternative to treat the deficiency, but injections may also be used. Anemia alone cannot however explain the symptoms associated with vampirism, but anemia is a common symptom caused by other illnesses. Illnesses that have been connected to vampirism are porphyria, rabies, and pellagra.

Rabies is probably the disease that has been associated with vampires the longest. As early as 1733, a theory started to spread. The theory was that people who had contracted the rabies virus were at higher risk of becoming undead. During this time, rabies was a relatively common disease. Rabies is a viral infection that spreads through saliva and the most common way to be infected is to be bitten by a rabid animal. The first symptoms of having the virus is fatigue, a general feeling of illness, temporary numbness and fever. Later the rabies will cause the carrier to become hydrophobic, meaning that they are instinctively afraid of water. Those inflicted will also suffer spasms and difficulty sleeping. Sudden outbursts and biting can occur too, which will spread the rabies to a new host. The irrational outbursts are due to an inflammation of the nerves in the brain. According to some folklore, vampires cannot cross bodies of water, which is why rabies has been associated with vampirism since the most well known and most obvious sign of rabies is a fear of water. Using water on a person was also thought to be a way to stop a transformation into a vampire. A parallel to this is that the vampire does not have a mirror reflection. The person suffering from rabies can not drink water and the mere presence of it can cause spasms and bloody coughing. Even the mirror image in water may trigger the reaction, which would explain the myth of the vampire lacking a mirror image. The sufferer simply avoids it entirely. That the disease is spread through saliva also explains where the idea of vampires spreading vampirism through bites to the neck comes from. The difficulty sleeping may also explain the myth of being active at night.

After anemia, porphyria is the most common disease to be associated with vampirism. It is a hereditary disease that may come in many forms. The most common one is acute intermittent porphyria (AIP). All porphyria diseases are very uncommon, but more common in northern Sweden that the south.

A contributing factor of why the illness breaks out may be physical and/or psychological stress, but also sex hormone abnormalities. Symptoms of AIP are strong abdominal pains that may lead to vomiting. The sufferer may also experience muscle weakness, numbness and cramps. Psychological symptoms may be insomnia and depression. The most obvious tell of AIP, however, is red colored urine. Another variant of porphyria is porphyria cutanea tarda (PCT). Symptoms of PCT are increased sensitivity to light that can result in blisters and fragile skin. In the most severe cases of porphyria, the treatment is a transplant of blood or bone marrow. Congenital erythropoietic porphyria (CEP), is both the most rare and aggressive form of porphyria. It is also the most common form to be associated with vampirism. The sensitivity to light is so extreme that is causes the sufferer's skin to become inflamed and causes anemia. In addition to skin damage, it may also damage cartilage and bone. This may lead to disfigurement of the eyelids, nose and fingers. The teeth can also discolor and get a red and brown shade. Porphyria may also cause the gums to retract, and causing the illusion of having bigger teeth.

Many misunderstandings, exaggerations and myths exist surrounding the connection between porphyria and our perception of the vampire. Even though several symptoms may fit, conformation bias can take over. We may only see what fits the image of vampirism, and disregard other, equally important, facts.

The connection between vampirism and porphyria began in 1982 when Dr David H. Dolphin, a biochemist, wrote an article in which he suggested that a connection existed. The statement spread and in 1985, he presented his theory at the annual meeting for *American Association for the Advancement of Science*. Dolphin meant that, with the previously stated symptoms as reference, that both the vampire and werewolf myths may come from humans suffering from porphyria. That is, our forefathers probably mistook porphyria for vampirism. The news spread quickly byt instead in bringing clarity, the media reported instead that the sufferers of porphyria were vampires. This has caused further suffering to those who already suffered from porphyria and thet did not wish to be further associated with vampirism. Afterwords, Dolphin has recieved criticism for his claim, deeming it irresponsible.

Some critics posited that Dolphin should have published a scientific article on the subject first, instead of making a public statement that reached millions of readers. The paper wrote that these 'vampires' compensated their lack of blood by drinking the blood of others. Media sources also wrote that carriers of the genes that cause the illness could become infected after a traumatic event, like the loss of blood. That is, if you carried these genes and were bitten by someone with porphyria, it would then genetically trigger the onset of the illness in you. It is, however, not possible to compensate anemia with drinking someone else's blood.

Ann Cox, at McGill University, wrote in a scientific article from 1995 (*Porphyria and Vampirism: Another Myth in the Making*), that because a human cannot absorb nutrients from blood that has been drunk, would make this self-medication meaningless as a treatment. She stated that the illness may have caused the sick to take desperate measures. Moreover, since it is primarily the rarest variant of porphyria that matches the image of the vampire, it has also been questioned how reasonable it is that all those suspected of being vampires really suffered from that disease.

Porphyria is a very uncommon diseasem but with our current ability of self-diagnosing through a quick search on the internet, the consequences can be catastrophic. The sick then risk being normalized within the framework of the subculture. However, it is not just vampirism that largely resembles the symptoms of porphyria. The symptoms can also relate to the werewolf myth. In a medical journal from 1964, the author L. Illis, wrote an article named *On Porphyria and the Etiology of Werewolves*, where the author claims that the majority of cases of 'werewolves' have suffered from porphyria.

As mentioned before, porphyria is inheritable, which means that they may be dormant without breaking out. Triggering factors may be increased production on sex hormones or stress, both physical and mental. This is an interesting coincidence because the 'awakening' of a vampire is said to happen during puberty. Vampirism is also said to be hereditary or transmitted through a bite. Being bitten by another human being shoul, reasonably, be both physically and mentally taxing, and could thus be, theoretically, a triggering factor for someone carrying porphyria. In this case, it is plausible, that families with porphyria in their genes believed it to be vampirism.

Likely, not all self-described vampirists have either porphyria or anemia, but it is difficult to disregard the similarities with the supposed symptoms of vampirism. It is understandable that the symptoms of these illnesses may have been frightful for our forefathers, since they lacked medical understanding.

Scientists have looked closer at other illnesses that may explain the emergence of the vampire mythology, and by extension, the vampirists of our time. This was because of the controversy surrounding the connection of vampirism and porphyria. One of them is pellagra, and it is said to be consistent with the symptoms associated with vampirism. Pellagra is the deficiency of the vitamin niacin. The deficiency was first discovered in 1735 and is called the 4D-disease. Meaning, diarrhea, dementia, dermatitis and death. Dermatitis causes sun sensitivity and the sun may cause inflammation of the skin. The skin may become thich, red, to scale and blister. The tongue can also swell and get a red color. The dementia may show itself through having trouble sleeping and acting aggressively. Dementia can also lead to refusal to eat, whoch in combination with diarrhea can result in malnourishment. Pellagra can also result in death, which may happen suddenly and without warning.

Rabies, porphyria and pellagra all have symptoms that may explain the behavior and appearance of the vampires in the 1700's. None can however explain them in full. Our ignorance of how bodies behave post mortem may have often been the sources for the growth of vampiric mythologies.

Chapter 2

To Define the Vampirist

'I turned and he was leaning toward me, his pale, glorious face just inches from mine.'

(From the book *Twilight* by Stephenie Meyer)

ON VAMPIRIST WEBSITES, the symptoms of vampirism are often lifted. They differ from site to site, but blood deficiency, bigger canine teeth, photosensitivity and red urine are some of the alleged symptoms. How do you then recognize a vampirist and how does vampirism affect everyday life? The condition involves a variety of symptoms, but they differ from what we have seen in movies and read in literature.

In addition to the definition, the spelling is a topic being discussed, which encompasses the English 'vampire' and 'vampyre', respectively. The vampirists who prefer to be called 'vampyres', often refer to a desire to distinguish the true vampires from the vampires in fiction. A 'vampyre' is thus the real vampire of our time, unlike the supernatural being found in film and outher fiction. Researchers in the field suggest the term 'vampirist' to be used when referring to a human who engages in vampirical activities.

Popular Culture and Vampirists

It was when popular culture incorporated the vampire into fiction that the widespread fear of them and associated superstition began to decline. Since then, the vampire has been associated with fiction and not something that gave rise to real horror.

How the vampire has been portrayed in popular culture is also something that has, to say the least, changed over time. We went from Bram Stokers *Dracula*, first printed in 1897, to Stephenie Meyers Twilight series, which started with *Twilight* in 2005. Stoker's Count Dracula was the prince of darkness. Edward, and the other vampires, in the Twilight universe sparkle instead in sunlight. Is should be added that Bram Stoker was not the first to write pure fiction about vampires, but his book is the earliest example that has been widely spread. Apart from folk lore and early urban legends, the vampire in literature can be traced to the poem *The Vampire* from 1748 by the German poet Heinrich August Ossenfelder. There are several early examples of poetry dripping with vampire lore. The first fictional novel on the theme may be John William Polidori's *The Vampyre* from 1819. An early, popular vampire movie is the German silent movie *Nosferatu* from 1922, directed by Friedrich Willhelm Murnau, but there are even earlier examples. These are however difficult to find, which makes it even more difficult to determine which one was the earliest vampire movie. A possible candidate is the German *A Night of Horror* from 1916. Today the market has exploded, and the vampire fan never needs to be bored.

Vampirists of Our Time

Vampires in films are often portrayed as night-active creatures, and spend the day in comfort and safety, resting in their coffins. But how well does this picture match vampirists and how do you know if someone is one? Perhaps there are reasons to suspect if the person in question constantly wears sunglasses, gets easily tanned and looks almost rudely young for their age. There exists a flurry of lists to check off is vampirism is suspected, thus, opinions are split as to what the state means and what criteria to be met. Commonly occurring characteristics to look out for are:

- ❖ Pale skin
- ❖ Prefers dark environments
- ❖ Needs blood to feel good
- ❖ Large and pointy canines
- ❖ Youthful appearance

Like popular culture, inspired by folk lore and myths to create the vampire of fiction, has the vampirists also been influenced by the ideas of popular culture. This means that our definitions of what a vampire is also affects how these people choose to live their lives. Research has also shown that consumption of popular culture can affect our perception of what is possible. The study, published in 2006, was conducted by Williams, Robbins and Picton at the University of Wales. The sample consisted of 1133 young people, aged 13 to 15, who were asked to answer several questions in a questionnaire. The students answered how many hours of television they watched every day, and if they believed if vampires existed or not. More youths who watched television for more than four hours every day, answered that they believed in vampires, compared to youths who watched less television. Since it is only a single study, however, it is not possible to make any definite conclusions based on the results, as there are several unexplored variables that may have affected the results.

The Pale Skin

In popular culture, the sun has long been the Achilles' heel of the vampire, which has pushed the unfortunate to a life away from all that resembles community. For the Count in question, a sunshine holiday would be a suicide mission. But if vampirism is to be incorporated into the everyday life of a person, perhaps the story may have to be rewritten. Many vampirists agree that pale skin and sensitivity to light are characteristic features. However, there is no mention of fire or turning to ash when exposed to sunlight.

The vampirists skin is easily tanned, and the eyes are often light-sensitive. An easy way to remedy the situation is to regularly use a sunscreen and wear sunglasses. Another risk are migraines, with dizziness, and nausea as consequences. Unprotected skin can feel blistering hot. With the sensitivity to sunlight, many prefer the cool embrace of the shadows. Through this, the aging effect of UV radiation is avoided, which some claim is the reason to the youthful appearance of vampirists. Not being exposed to unnecessary stress from the sun has its advantages, and some also think it is possible to increase the tolerance for sunlight to cope with it better. In this way, the negative consequences can be avoided, and a normal life is possible. The author Carol Page has met the vampirist Misty. Misty calims to have a strong sensitivity to light that results in discomfort if the stays in the sun for too long. Misty is also anemic. She uses sunscreen daily and claims that she has previously fainted a number of times because of the heat. She also wears sunglasses to protect her sensitive eyes. When she drinks human blood, she experiences that she is better at coping with the light for a few days. People who claim to be both vampirists and anemic may sometimes claim that iron supplements do not remedy the illness, but that they feel better after ingesting blood. Misty claims that iron supplements upset her stomach and therefore does not want to taket hem, even though she is anemic. Page writes that Misty seems to want to maintain her anemic condition. Another vampirist, calling himself Vlad, claims that he got third-degree burns after spendning an hour in the sun. Because of the sensitivity to light, he seeks to protect himself when he is outdoors, he also always wears sunglasses.

The eyes can also differ from that of humans. A common perception is that the iris is surrounded by a dark ring and has a lighter color just around the pupil. There are also theories that the vampirist develops completely black eyes, especially when the need for blood is not satisfied. The dark eyes also fill the function of having night vision. This ability could be useful when it's hunting time, because where do predators hunt best, if not in the dark?

Fangs

An attribute, apart from blood consumption, may be what is most intimately associated with vampires, are oversized and sharp canines. There is, however, no consensus among vampirists whether fangs exist or not. Those who embrace a more extravagant view assert that it is an associated detail – natural as well as artificial. Some claim that the vampirist by nature has larger canine teeth, while others insert more or less permanent implants. For those who are incidentally interested in acquiring a pair of fangs for themselves can, for example, turn to the dental sculptor, and vampirist, Father Sebastiaan, who manufactures individually adapted removable teeth. His teet hare said to last for several years and he also makes sure that the implants match the shade of the client's natural teeth. Sebastiaan has previously worked as a dentist and has also written several books on occultism and vampirism. Another option is to sharpen the natural teeth. Critics, on the other hand, argue that it is a myth that is based on the idea of the vampire as an evil predator. From this perspective, the sharp canines are an example of prejudice derived from fiction in the form of literature and film.

Fangs also remind us of the appearance of a predator, and some vampirists claim that they are able to grow fangs when it is time to eat. Being able to extend and retract their fangs with willpower is not an argument that can be supported by science, since there must forst be a genetic mutation for it to be possible. With today's research, we know which processes are theoretically based on immortal cells, but the processes behind an addition of cells that allow for growing teeth rapidly are something completely different.

How about food and drinking habits? Rarely do we see vampires in movies eating a regular meal. If vampirism is to work outside of film, the dietary needs to be expanded. Vampirists today rarely say that they survive on blood alone. If the blood supply dwindles, there are plenty of, more or less likely, substitutes that are said to redemy the thirst. You'll find more information about these habits in the chapter *Blood Drinking Vampirists*.

Clothing

There are many of us who can recognize ourselves in the situation of having a wardrobe full of clothes, yet nothing to wear. But there are those who have it worse. If you do not have a mirror image and are invisible in photographs, how do you then decide on what to wear and how it fits? Are the colors in harmony with one and other or is it a complete mismatch? An alternative is to let a friend paint you, as in the scene of the mockumentary, *What we do in the Shadows*, but with such a long process, there are likely very few balls being held at the castle.

In the case of clothing, it is primarily the Gothic clothing style that dominates the preconceptions of the vampire. Many are, however, critical of that image being considered vampire-like as it is associated with being somewhat gloomy, dangerous and macabre. The vampirist does not want to be associated with a terrifying figure, hiding behind a cape at the edges of society and attacks their victims when they least expect it.

The truth is that there is no absolute code of how to dress. It is therefore up to personal preference – even if you are a vampirist.

The sensitivity to sunlight has a close connection with the vampires sleeping habits. Today's vampirists usually do not sleep in coffins, although dark and soundproofed environments are sometimes preferred. Therefore, the image of the vampire being trapped in its coffin does not align very well with reality. Most live a seemingly normal life. They have regular jobs, wear regular clothing and sleep i regular beds. However, there are a few who prefer a coffin, saying that they enjoy the sound-proof environment.

Although some argue that the vampirist can live a completely normal life, many have the perception that the night gives them a sharper altertness. It can make it difficult to cope with day-to-day life full of studies or work, resulting in working after everyone else goes to bed which is preferable in many cases.

The explanation for night activity is said to be that the reaction to light and dark are biologically different. Melatonin is the hormone that usually makes us tired when the night falls, but that function does not work for these pople.

Because of the sensitivity to heat, cooler environments, especially where they sleep, is also prefered. Since sleeping occurs during daytime, buying dark roller blinds is a good investment to help keep the temperature down in the bedroom.

Holy Symbols

Is it possible to keep the vampirist at a distance with the help of garlic at the front door, silver items and a crucifix in the back pocket? Like with many other aspects, here there are also separate opinions, but many agree that the answer is no to the questions above. However, because of the mere developed senses, they tend to be better at distinguishing and recognizing smells and scents. Garlic has quite a sharp smell to it and can thus be perceived as uncomfortable by some, but not harmful in any way.

The negative impact of touching a crucifix is a myth sprung from the idea that vampires are godforsaken creatures. No other religious objects or symbols trigger any reaction, either. In the chapter *Religious Vampirists*, certain vampire religions will be brought up, but many testify that a certain belief is not automatically linked with vampirism. As a vampirist, you can therefore be anything from an atheist to devil worshiper. Against this background, it is natural that religious symbols do not affect these counts of darkness.

Life Span and Disease Resistance

The perceptions regarding life expectancy and (im)mortality are highly varied. It is alleged that the vampirist lives as long as a human to others who say they can live for hundreds of years. Regarding the latter, there is also a variation in theories whether they reincarnate or live in the same body throughout their lifetime. The slightly more balanced view is that, thanks to their slower aging process, they can live approximately twenty years longer, compared to humans. Many seem to agree that, regardless of age, they always look younger, as previously mentioned, which may be related to the avoidance of the sun's harmful radiation.

What about disease resistance? Is a vampirist immune to human illnesses? On one hand, some say that the condition protects against diseases through a stronger immune system, whole others are doubt that claim. Those who claim immortality of the vampirist tend to also make claims about disease resistance.

There are those who claim that they possess a strenght, stronger healing ability, and resilience far beyond that of humans. In exceptional cases, it is claimed that their bodies are able to regenerate lost organs and parts of the body. This also means that the vampirist has more opportunities to survive severe injuries and that they do not suffer pain as easily. A basic premise for this to be possible is that the vampirist receives a sufficient amount of blood. However, skeptical vampirists refer to the fact that they are basically a human being and that such perceptions can be dangerous as they may result in unnecessary risk taking.

The vampire has gone from being a monstrous figure with its residence in the shadows to an elegant figure with exceptional abilities. It's more of a role model than anything else, so it's no wonder that people want to identify themselves as vampirists. It may be possible that it is the thought of eternal youth that attracts. Mecial developments are all very well, but with more knowledge, awareness of our vulnerability has also increased. Today, even aging is something that can be remedied. The fact that our bodies are aging reminds us of our own inevitable death.

Research has been conducted in the area of immortal cells. Human aging is due to an ongoing cell division and a cell can only be divided a number of times before it dies. Tests have been performed on mice, which showed that the mice that ate 30 percent less than the control group, lived on average of 56 months instead of the normal 39. The downside of the diet was that the slow aging process increased to risk of cancer.

In February 2017, the Swedish magazine Veckans Affärer reported that the researcher Aubrey de Gray (1963-) argues that in the future it will be possible to stop aging. He perceives aging as a disease that can be cured, meaning that science and technology is the key.

Nowadays, vampirists are not referred to as undead beings, but there are theories that they can live longer than humans. Vampirists certainly need to eat a varied diet of regular food, but some claim that they eat less than other pople. The reason is said to be that they get so much life force through, for example, blood. Theoretically, this could mean that the vampirist has fewer free radicals in their bodies. Because of this, the cells of the body are not divided at the same rate. Perhaps the blood drinking vampirist has solved the mystery of prolonging life.

(An Attempt at a) Conclusion

Is the vampirist a species of its own or is it a human with very particular desires? Today's vampirists seem to have more in common with humans than the zombie-like monsters that rose from their graves in the 18th century. Even so, there are still vampirists who think they are a separate species that developed alongside humans. An alternative view is that it is a natural result of evolution. From this perspective, human beings will eventually go extinct, and be replaced by our more evolved relative, vampirists. So, what is a vampirist? There are probably as many answers to the question as there are self-appointed vampirists. The self-appointed vampirist Izidari (blogger and writer), argues that many websites spread false information and have criteria that are too wide, which leads to many believing they are vampirists, then in fact, they are not.

Joseph Laycock, is a writer and a PhD professor of religion at Texas State University. He believes that what distinguishes a vampirist is the desire for blood and in the case of withdrawal, the unpleasant symptoms. There are also those who further branch out the concept by identifying different forms of vampirism. The most common division is based on whether the vampirist gets energy through blood or through mental means (psychic vampirism). The state is therefore not synonymous with drinking blood and all consumption of blood is also not considered to fall within the framework of vampirism. The closest to a consensus that can be made in the world of vampires is that the vampirist is a being in human form that survives through taking blood or energy from something och someone else. In some cases, the blood is only one form of energy, while others claim that their bodies suffer from a physiological anemia. Human, including vampirists, are diverse and can thus not be easily compartmentalized.

Chapter 3

Clinical Vampirism

'Dr. Seward will believe I'm not insane!'

(From the movie *Dracula: Dead and loving it*, 1995)

THE FRENCH PHILOSOPHER Michel Foucault (1926 - 1984) wrote the book *History of Madness* which was first published in 1961. The book describes how mental illness was constructed by distinguishing the 'insane' group from what we call normal behavior.

Clinical vampirism is a disputed condition. The disease is currently not a diagnosis in either the DSM-V or ICD-10, but it is impossible not to encounter the concept when studying vampirism. An alternative and somewhat playful diagnoses is Renfield's Syndrome. I was Richard Noll (1959-), an American medical historian and psychologist who coined the expression in 1992 and pointed out that the symptoms associated with the disease are reminiscentof Renfield, a character in Bram Stoker's *Dracula*. The diagnosis is also included in his book *The Encyclopedia of Schizophrenia and Other Psychotic Disorders*, published in 2007.

If a self-indentified vampirist wishes to be declared sick or not, I will leave unsaid. Depending on the attitude of the condition of oneself, the views are likely to vary widely. How outsiders view the matter is probably also very different. Everything is in what we perceive as normal and what are deviations that should be diagnosed. When we diagnose something, a distancing happens also. The limits of what has been considered normal have also changed throughout the ages.

Definition of the Disease

Because vampirism is not included in any official diagnostic manual, there are varying interpretations of the meaning of the term. However, it is a rare condition and one of the earliest attempts to document the condition was made by Richard von Krafft-Ebing (1840-1902). His classic work *Psychopathia Sexualis* from 1886 was considered obscure and was kept locked away from the public by librarians. Krafft-Ebing was a German neurologist, and in the book, he described 238 cases of norm breaking sexuality. He does not name the condition 'clinical vampirism', but in the section for sadism he describes several cases where the perpetrator has been sexually excited by blood. Krafft-Ebing linked vampirism to sexuality and power. He realized that the feeling of power was closely associated with the presence of blood and that it thus seemed to be power that gave rise to pleasure. The earlier mentioned psychologist Richard Noll is in the same line of thinking as he summarizes clinical vampirism as a blood fetisch that gives the affected a compulsive, often sexual, need to drink blood.

Blood is probably the first thing many think about when vampirism is being discussed. But, in accordance with the definition of the term, British professor Herschel Prins (1928-2016) posits that the drinking of blood is not always there. Herschel Prins claimed in hos 1980's research that the condition could be expressed in many ways and he divided vampirism into four different categories which can be summarized as follows:

* Necrosadistic vampirism: Blood consumption, sexual arousal over blood, necrophilia and necrosadism.
* Necrophilia: Sexual arousal over dead bodies, but blood consumption does not occur.
* Vampirism: Sexual arousal by drinking the blood of another person.
* Autovampirism: Sexual arousal by drinking ones own blood.

Prins therefore argued for a close connection to necrophilia and sexual arousal, something that has been criticized. It is especially his focus on necrophilia that is questioned, as many see it as a completely different disorder. In particular, it has been debated whether necrophilia without the consumption of blood can be regarded as vampirism. The sexual arousal is always present, according to Prins' classification, but as several studies described below show, sexual excitement is something that is often absent.

In a South African research study from 2006 by Gubb, Segal, Khota and Dicks, the authors argue that even psychic vampirism should be included in the concept. They base this on the finding that people affected by it show similar symptoms. They claim that vampirism can occur when someone has an unclear concept of self, where the boundary between the self and the surroundings is blurry. It can lead to beliefs that one has the ability to absorb the strength and abilities of other people.

Link to Other Diseases

The researchers Jaffé and DiCataldo have investigated the relationship between vampirism, schizophrenia, and psychopathic personality disorder. They claim that people with schizophrenia can experience dissociation in relation to the self. To see their own blood can then serve as a confirmation of their own existence. If the affected has traits of psychopathy or antisocial personality disorder, the illness may exoress itself differently. These tend to be more prone to acting out and vampirism is closely linked with the sense of having control over other people. In these cases, the condition may have dire consequences.

There is a study by Hemphill and Zabov, arguing that the three main symptoms of clinical vampirism are compulsive consumption of blood, identity problems and a great interest in death that goes beyond mere curiosity. However, their research shows that the vast majority of vampirists are uninterested by the occult, lack any illnesses that include psychosis, and that the blood has no sexual meaning. Some act out violently, while others turn the violent behavior on oneself.

Both studies showed that people with clinical vampirism have a normal level of intelligence. It was also found that sexual arousal related to blood was not something that stood out. In fact, several of those who participated in the study considered themselves asexual. Herschel Prins' study is in stark contrast to these conclusions. He found that the affected people are intellectually and emotionally underdeveloped. Prins' reasoning that it is likely the presence of schizophrenia that causes the underdevelopment. Intelligence can certainly be defined in different ways and it is possible that it simply is a case of conceptual confusion or different views of mental illness.

Early Symptoms

Richard Noll believes that the symptoms of vampirism often appear in early childhood. For example, the child may have been involved in a sexual situation where blood has been present. The disease progression then takes place gradually and the fascination with blood intensifies during the teenage years. The teen begins to drink their own blood, but when their own blood no longer satisfies their desire, the person progresses to drinking blood from other people. The blood thirst is of a compulsive nature, and the disease also includes the belief of being a vampire herself. In some cases, it goes so far that the person commits murder to gain access to the strengthening energy of the blood. An early fascination with blood can, in some cases, result in cruelty to animals, as seen in several studies.

The Influence of Childhood

In many case studies of clinical vampirism, violence or neglect during childhood has been noted, or strong aversion to the parents. There are, however, also examples of studies that show the opposite, that childhood has not been conspicuously dramatic. However, it is common to see signs early on in childhood that something is not right. The reason for it is unclear and there are many different explanatory models. In some cases, it appears to be a traumatic event that triggered the drive, while in other cases there is no obvious triggering factor.

Researcher Neil Wilson has conducted a study in America with a focus on psychic vampirism. The article does not mention the concept of clinical vampirism, but Wilson speaks instead of vampiric transferring. He believes that important relationships in early childhood are transmitted to other people and affect relationships later in life. From this point of view, vampirism could be regarded as a form of relationship bonding. By taking energy from other people, alternatively drinking their blood, the vampirist comes close to other people in a way that is not possible otherwise. In light of what is stated above, Wilson suggested in his study that (psychic) vampirism may be triggered because of an upbringing characterized by self-sufficiency. The child learns to 'suck the life force' from its surroundings. Even the opposite can occur, as the now adult child instead seeks a dominant partner who maintains the power hierarchy.

Case Studies of Clinical Vampirism

In a Malaysian case study from Phang, Kayatri, and Ang, from 2013, the connection between clinical vampirism and schizophrenia, and antisocial personality disorder was investigated. The woman in the study bit her own tongue several times a week to drink the blood, she also used syringes. She stated that she had previously hurt other people, but that this helped her to function normally. The urge had been with her already as a child, but in puberty, and having periods, her need had increased. She experienced symptoms such as anxiety, restlessness, sensitivity to light and hair loss when she did not get enough blood. When she was five years old, her father began to assault her mother, and the authors of the study connect her thirst for blood with her traumatic childhood. The desire for blood coincided with times when she felt alone. They posit that she was exposed to blood at an early stage and that the blood for her represented the family ties she wanted to mend. In summary, the authors of the study claim that the woman represents a case of autovampirism and that the condition does not necessarily have to be connected with other mental illnesses. Vampirism can simply be a symptom of the desire to feel a context and love – something that most people strive for.

Another case study shows a case where clinical vampirism occurred later in life. The study is from 2012 and was conducted by Sakarya, Gunez, Ozturk and Sar. They investigated the relationship between vampirism and diagnoses such as Dissociative Identity Disorder (DID) and Post Traumatic Stress Disorder (PTSD). The study presents a case study of a man who has been drinking blood for the past three years. The time coincided with the death of his daughter. Earlier, the man's uncle had been murdered. He had been close to the body, touched it and felt the smell of is blood. He had also witnessed a murder where a friend cut off another man's head and penis. After a clinical interview, he was diagnosed with DID. Tests also showed signs of alcohol abuse, PTSD and depression. However, the criteria for schizophrenia were not met.

A Separate Diagnosis?

In his book, *Bizarre Behaviours,* from 1990, Herschel Prins outlines one of his studies conducted from May 1983 to February 1984. The study included only professionals in the field; primarily psychiatrists and a few anthropologists. Prins used a questionnaire that he sent out to a total of 51 people, of which he received 45 replies. What Prins wanted to find out was to what extent they encountered vampirism in their daily work and what their professional assessment of the condition was.

Of the 34 psychiatrists, 33 said that vampirism was likely linked to other psychiatric conditions. The most common connection was schizophrenia, but severe personality disorder and developmental disturbances were also common. Only two of Prins' respondents reported cases where they themselves had encountered clinical vampirism. Prins, however, argues that vampirism may be more common than we think, since it is likely that many sufferers are not inclined to come forward and disclose their behavior. It is also not clear that the sufferer is experiencing her condition as problematic.

Following the study, Prins came into contact with other professionals who shared their experiences with vampirists. One of them reported as many as five cases, all of whom were patients in mental health care. They were all suspected of suffering from some form of personality disorder. A woman was convinced that her canines grew, and she was turning into a vampire. A 19-year-old man stabbed an older widower as practice before a great sacrificial ritual. The planned ritual included a 13-year-old boy who would give him youth and eternal life. During his trial, it was found that he used to dress as Count Dracula and that he was a frequent visitor of cemeteries.

In summary, it is difficult to give an answer as to whether vampirism should be seen as a diagnosis or if it may be a component in other psychiatric conditions. Perhaps the answer to the question is not that simple. It seems that vampirism can have several different causes and there is also a variety in how vampirism is expressed.

Today's research in the area of clinical vampirism is rare, but most of the studies have shown that other mental problems are often present, especially schizophrenia. Self-identified vampirists often express that they have felt alone in childhoos and have difficulty forming relationships. The blood consumption and the relationship to a donor then becomes a substitute for the close ties that the person may have difficulty forming.

In cases where vampirism does not hurt the individual or the environment, it is doubtful whether it should be considered a diagnosis. Of course, there may be unprocessed experiences which in turn has resulted in such a survival strategy. Thus, when vampirism is merely a symptom of something else that is not quite right, focus should be on finding and treating the root cause of the problem.

I also want to emphasize that the aforementioned studies are extreme. Most vampirists never become subjects for research as they are well functioning members of society. It is thus only the most severe cases that are noted and there are often other psychiatric problems present. Theses cases are also often people who have committed particularly brutal violent crimes and through their actions harm their environment.

Chapter 4

'Vampire drag' and Vampirology

'I think we drink virgin blood because it sounds cool'

(From the movie *What we do in the shadows*, 2014)

THE VAMPIRE HAS HISTORICALLY been regarded as a creature at the edge of society living in seclusion from other people. However, modern depictions of vampires in literature and movies show that vampirism is compatible with a fully functioning everyday life. Move vampires can go to school, have friends and get a job. So what is the community like for todays vampirists? Human are a social animal. We are dependent on each other in many ways to cope and in most cases, we live together with some or a few fellow humans. If the vampirist is basically a human, then the same should apply to these individuals.

Great courage is required to be open of ones' vampirist identity, when you consider the imminent risk of being met with skepticism and ridicule. It is probably not a coincidence that much of the vampirist community today is on the internet. The step of 'coming out' as a vampirist is certainly less daunting when it can be done with the safety of anonymity.

It is unknown how many people in the world identify themselves as vampirists. Most likely they are a minority. An easy way to find like-minded people is to scour the internet. On the world wide web, you can finns almost anything; even forums that are directed directly to vampirists. A large part of the communication between vampirists seems to be through internet forums, although physical meetups can of course also take place. An example of a website that offers solid information for the inquisitive vampirist is the *Real Vampires Support Page*. Another example can be found on the *Sanguinarius* internet forum.

There also exists certain 'vampire houses', which is a group of vampirists with similar values and worldview. Often, the various vampire houses also have a closed internet forum that is open to their members only. Most do not have a physical headquarters, but only exist on the internet. Vampire houses have been criticized by some, because they assert that true vampirists act individually and not in groups. *Scarlet Moon Organization* is a vampire house that existed between 1999-2002 and aimed to be a meeting place for vampirists. The group mainly existed online, but they also organized meetings in person. One of their plans was to buy a property and rent rooms to their members. The group focused on blood drinking vampirists and did not have any religious orientation. On their website it was also possible to order various aids for extracting blood, such as knives and scalpels. They also provided information about recommended techniques. Unlike *Scarlet Moon*, many vampire houses define their world view and more information abour some them can be found in the chapter *Religious Vampirists*.

If the vampirist keeps her identity secret and conceals her condition, then the 'lifestyle vampirist' can be said to be its complete opposite. Lifestylers can be described as people embracing the vampire lifestyle. They like to play up the stereotype of what a vampire is and often have a gothic style. It also happens that they are referred to as 'vampire drag'. As the name suggests, it is about people who like to exaggerate the classic vampire myth – and do not shy away from showing it. Lifestyle vampires often receive strong criticism from those who cinsider themselves to know better and who claim to be genuine. The critics believe that they discredit true vampirists and spread prejudices.

Both lifestyle vampire and vampirists can engage in the consumption of blood. What separated them is the reason for the consumption. A vampirist claims to need blood to maintain good health, the lifestyle vampire chooses to drink blood to spice up everyday life. Many of the lifestyle vampires also do not think that vampires really exist, so they do not claim to be one. For the lifestyle vampire, blood consumption becomes a part of the caricature instead; of the role it plays. In a way, it could be compared to a person who participates in a role-playing group and a person who believes to be a real reincarnation of Gollum.

If the vampirists differ from how the everyday person imagines the caricature, then the picture probably matches the way a lifestyle vampire looks. It is not uncommon with cape, dark clothes, pale faces, fangs and contact lenses. Often, the style of the lifestyle vampire's choice of furniture is characterized by the Gothic style. Some lifestyle vampires, but also vampirists, even have their natural teeth grinded. An alternative is to purchase individually customizable detachable fangs. As mentioned earlier, for example, Father Sebastiaan, a trained dental technician, manufactures fangs for vampire fans. There is also a special piercing that is popular with the lifestyle vampires. The piercing is put under the skin of the throat with two red bumps on each side, all because it should resemble a classic vampire bite. A lifestyle vampire may also prefer to spend the night in a coffin instead of a soft bed.

What is the difference between a lifestyle vampire and a 'vampabee'? The crucial difference between them is that the former is completely aware that they are not, nor wish to be, a vampirist. They only have a penchant for the vampire lifestyle. A vampabee may think it's a vampirist, and it's not uncommon for this to be publicly disclosed. For the vampabee, the desire to be a real vampirist is so strong that the person can even start to believe it. Often the vampabee is drawn to vampirist circles, as a groupie. For many vampirists, it is in their nature to keep a low profile and not try to attract too much attention. If someone continually claims to be a vampirist and seems desperate to convince his surrounding, it may be a sign that the person in question is a vampabee.

Researching Vampirologists

A lot of people are skeptical of the existence of vampirists, and some even go so far as to claim that they are sick people with delusions. There are also websites dedicated to disproving the vampirist's existence, such as the website *Vampires Are Not Real.* Life as a vampirist is certainly not easy. They often experience the need to conceal their identity, and there are also those lifestyle vampires that creats confusion in the public. Vampirists therefore have a lot to prove and this is where our vampirologists play an important role.

Most researchers within vampire domains work from medical diagnoses explaining the symptoms that self-appointed vampirists say they experience. However, there also exists another branch of 'research' – vampirists, or vampire fans, seeking scientific answers to issues related to the condition. They simply assume that vampirists exist, which means that both research methods and results look a little different. Often the focus is on finding evidence of the existence of the vampirist, finding out how many there are, and charting how their lives are. It is not about basic research, but rather heavily biased. The interest in finding out more about vampirism has also resulted in the creation of several groups. They call themselves vampirologists.

Queens Vampire Research Center

The *Queens Vampire Research Center* is said to have been founded in 1823 and its headquarters is said to be located in Bucharest, Romania. The research center's funding is dependent on donations and they have a lab where different types of experiments and tests can be performed. Their latest project is about finding a cure for vampirism. The Center also performs autopsies on commission if there are questions surrounding a person's cause of death. They are very secretive and do not allow for transparency from third parties. For example, there are no pictures from the Center on the website. They instead use photos from environments that are said to be similar to theirs. Of course, it also makes it difficult to assess the truth and credibility of their alleged activites. The purpose of the research is to find evidence of the existence of the vampirist and also a biological explanation that is scientifically substantiated. Furthermore, the Center declares that the vampirist is to be seen as essentially different from humans. This is due to the idea that they have completely different DNA structure in comparison with humans. The vampirist is not seen as a supernatural being, but rather as an improved human being. They say they hold evidence of all their theories, but to gain access to them, a visit to their office is required.

They argue that the only method of purely visually detecting a real vampirist is to witness the self-healing process. The Center believes that its ability to heal is very fast, so by inflicting the vampirist harm, it is possible to see this healing happen in front of the eyes of the experimenter, usually within a few minutes.

They are also said to have the ability to regenerate organs by adding blood from an external source. They further argue that the canine teeth are made up of a softer material that allows for storage inside the gums. Apparently, it should only take a few minutes to unfold the teeth.

On the website of the Center you can read about study object '12-04-XX'. In 2007, an autopsy of a body missing the heart was carried out, the autopsy included removal of the brain. The findings from the autopsy were that the deceased had a previously unknown blood group, and that the body decomposed very quickly. Mutated and unknown antibodies were claimed to be in the blood. The day after the autopsy, the body was mysteriously gone... typical, right?

The Count Dracula Fan Club

The Count Dracula Fan Club was founded in 1965 in New York by Dr Jeanne Keyes Youngson. In addition to research, the group also specializes in collecting vampire-related books and articles. In their library department, *Count Dracula Research Library*, there is said to be around 25,000 titles. The focus is on the popular culture vampire, and mainly on Bram Stokers *Dracula*. They say they have had over 5,000 members from twelve different countries between the ages of 12 and 83 years. The group offers support for anyone interested in the subject, but they also conduct their own studies.

During the period of February 1998 to March 1999, Youngson sent 933 polls, of which 713 were filled in. The survey was international and included a total of 23 countries. Of the 713 people who answered the survey, 272 were said to be vampirists, alternatively had made the claim earlier in life. The responses showed that those who drank blood got ahold of it through, for example, packaged meat, themselves or a friend, live animals, slaughterhouses, and more. Most people stated that their friends were not aware that they were vampirists and that their nature had not been a choice for them. Many used fangs often or sometimes and sunlight was also said to cause them discomfort. The majority did not think they were living longer than other people, and they did not experienced enhanced night vision. The study results also showed that 71 percent of the vampirists regularly drank blood.

Another study result is based on interviews conducted over an eleven-year period. All respondents believed to be vampirists or experienced an attraction for blood. Almost all the blood-drinking participants had a traumatic experience previously in their lives. One of the conclusions of the study was that there appeared to be a connection between a traumatic childhood and a strong need for warmth and proximity in adulthood – and for some, this desire is expressed in vampirism.

Vampire Research Center

The *Vampire Research Center* was founded in 1972 in New York by teacher Stephen Kaplan (1941 - 1995) who claimed to have examined vampirists since 1981. The Center's vampire research was conducted by Kaplan himself and his wife Roxanne Salch Kaplan, but it is said that experts in different areas were also involved. Kaplan claimed that he had constant contact with people who shared his interest for various reasons – they may have suspected they were themselves vampirists or they thought they had met someone who was. Kaplan has presented an overview of the various forms of vampirism that exist in subcultures; lifestyle vampires, blood fetishists, psychic vampirists as well as true vampirists. According to the Center, only the blood drinking vampirist is regarded as 'genuine'. During the 1980s three studies were also conducted, which consisted of forms sent to some of the people who contacted the Center over the years. The Center has concluded that there are about 600 true vampirists in the world and most live in California. The current lifestyle vampires were estimated to amount to about 1000. However, the selection in the studies was extremely limited, which means that the reliability of the Center's results should be considered as very low.

Norine Dresser

Norine Dresser is an American writer, anthropologist and folklorist. She is not part of any group, but has conducted her vampire studies on her own. One of her stuies consisted of three different surveys, one of which was addressed to students. Of these, 574 students answered, and the study included a total of 35 countries. Another focus group was porphyria patients, who were interviewed by telephone and mail. Finally, vampire fans recieved a third questionnaire, that group included people who themselves believed themselves to be vampirists. The research was conducted in 1986 and resulted in Dresser's book *American Vampires: fans, victims, practitioners* released in 1989 and showed that 27 percent of the students believed in vampires.

Speaking of the reliability of the collected answers, Dresser believes that regardless, the answers give an irreplaceable insight into the minds of those living as vampirists in their daily lives. However, if symptoms are faked or placebo, it still gives an interesting answer.

Atlanta Vampire Alliance

The *Atlanta Vampire Alliance* (AVA) is a small organization founded in 2005. There are only 13 members, of which five are also the founders of the house. The house has no hierarchy, but everyone is seen as equals. However, it is an elitist group that does not accept anyone. To be considered a potential member, you have to be 21 years or older, in good mental health and a spotledd criminal record is also required. Both blood drinking and psychic vampirists are welcome. The member engagement includes participation in the online discussion forum, attendance at various types of gatherings and to actively participate in the work on research projects. Every month a member meeting is also held. Although membership conditions are strictly limited, the group's Internet forum is completely open to anyone to use. Their ambition is to spread a greater understanding in society for what vampirism means and to provide a natural support for all the vampirists who feel lost. The group does not take a stand for or against any particular view of life or religion, nor are they attached to any particular vampire house.

Despite the modest membership count, the group has managed to build a reputation thanks to the surveys they have made. Research is central to the activities, and they have created the surveys *Vampire and Energy Work Research Survey* (VEWRS) and *Advanced Vampirism and Energy Work Research* (AVEWRS). Through the surveys they have collected a large amount of data revealing the vampirists' own thought about the condition and how vampirism affects the individual. The studies are available to read in full at their website *Suscitatio*.

Alienation and Affinity

For the vampirist who longs for a community, there seems to be many different forums and alternatives to consider. The fearsome loner of popular culture that lurks in the shadows seems to be passé.

Being a vampirist can for understandable reasons lead to a sense of loneliness and exclusion. It is, after all, a craving that most people may find difficult to recognize. Especially regarding the blood drinking vampirist. The drinking habits can give rise to both moral and ethical dilemmas, not to mention the stigma surrounding the matter. People who deviate from what we determined as normal are usually risked being seen as different, perhaps even mentally ill. Having an identity and feeling a sense of belongning to a community is central to many people, but what value we put in those terms varies. The subculture with vampirists offers a strong community of social exclusion as a common denominator. What deviates from the normal tends to be questioned, but by finding a community in the exclusion, cohesion can grow strong.

PART II

The Different Types of Vampirists

Chapter 5

How a Vampirist is Made

'I was born a vampire, as was every other member of this house. But you Frost … you were merely turned.'

(From the movie *Blade*, 1998)

IN POPULAR CULTURE, today, the transformation to vampire is often preceded by the classic bite. But unlike how the vampire is portrayed in literature and movies, not everyone agrees that it's a bite that's required to transform into a real vampirist. In fact, the biting is rejected by most. Many, instead, believe that it is a congenital condition, or something that happens through an active blood exchange. Another variant is reminiscent of a world view in which, through the study of holy writings, the vampirist achieves a higher rank, which in turn means that all can through practice and schooling become vampirists. Sometimes it's even about some form of occult ritual. Theories of that kind are found primarily in groups that market themselves as vampire religions or vampire houses.

Awakening

Whether vampirism is congenital or created, a so-called 'awakening' occurs. Awakening is the moment when the vampirist realizes her desire and potential new abilities. When this happens is contested. Some say it happens in connection with puberty, while others testify that they have been vampirists since childhood or even in middle age. Symptoms of puberty are a lot like a vampiric awakening, which means they can be difficult to distinguish.

The most significant change that awakening implies is probably the new desire that arises, a desire that can initially be difficult to define. Many testify that it feels like un unshakable thirst or a bottomless hunger. If the person in question has not read about vampirism, it may be difficult to realize its true nature. It is also far from everyone who identifies the source of desire, which can lead to a whole life of negative consequences. Common symptoms may, for example, be a feeling of fatigue that does not pass and a sensitivity to sunlight. Even the senses can be amplified, such as hearing and sense of smell. The common denominator is that the person in question gets rid of the negative symptoms when drinking blood alternatively absorbs energy.

An awakening seems to remind of equal parts puberty and withdrawal. The body changes rapidly, while showing clear signs of missing something vital.

Created Vampirism

For some, only the born vampirists are the real, others claim that genetic conditions have nothing to do with it. According to this theory, everyone can transform through a blood exchange with an active vampirist. Otherwise, theories are similar to each other purely practically; An active vampirist is thought to be able to transform someone by letting the person drink her blood. Many vampirists of this school, on the other hand, advise against carrying out a transformation and refer to the responsibility that implies and that it is hard to predict possible consequences. If the person in question has violent tendencies or suffers from mental health issues, it is said to be a pathway to trouble. Most people also fail to cope with the stress that a transformation implies and in view of the damage that may arise, the majority of vampirists choose to decline when they receive such requests. An explanation as to why it is this way may be because the theory can be easily disconfirmed. By refusing requests for a transformation with reference to the risks, the theory can not be disproven.

A Congenital Condition

It is a common belief that vampirism is a congenital condition and that it requires genetic conditions for awakening to occur. The innate vampirism can be activated by, for example, a blood exchange with an active vampirist. The person in question must therefore be born a vampirist, of which vampirism has been latent in the genetic material without breaking out. However, it is not only through a blood exchange a latent vampirism can be awakened. For some, the desire for blood is awakened after a traumatic event as a child where blood was central or after an accident with a knife.

Another theory is that sex hormones during puberty triggers vampirism. The proportion of people born with the ability to wake up is unclear, but some believe that most people have the prerequisites for it to happen.

A Vampirist's Own Words

Michelle Belanger, author and self-identified psychic vampirist, shares her story in the book *Vampires: In Their Own Words*.

Belanger tells that she discovered her vampiric nature in her teens, when she was isolated from her social circle. To give other people massages had always been something important for Belanger. She often offered to massage her friends, which was appreciated. When she moved in with her grandmother, she was separated from her friends unfortunately. It did not take long before Belanger experienced symptoms such as poorer immune system, palpitations, fatigue and dizziness. It was like a craving for something unknown that could not be extinguished no matter what she ate or drank. She let a doctor examine her, but the doctor could not find any cause for what she experienced.

Belanger's story resembles a classic case of depression due to isolation, which she herself considered. Belanger did not think that explanation was enough, but at first she did not accept that she was a vampirist. When the symptoms escalated, she also began to 'see' other people's energy fields, causing an irresistible urge within her. Belanger discovered that she negatively affected her environment because she now absorbed energy uncontrollably and without permission. Finally, she accepted her nature and was then burdened by strong guilt for what she exposed her environment to.

One more unusual theories, but also one of the most interesting, is that vampirism is caused by a particular virus. The most common term is HERV virus, but there are also similar theories where it is called Human Vampirism Virus (HVV) or V virus. Proponents reject the ideas that vampirism is due to energy shortage, instead, they mean that it is a change in the DNA structure or a genetic modification.

The condition involves changes in the brain's signaling substances and causes anemia in some organs such as the skin. In accordance with this theory, the intake of blood is also seen as the only true vampirism and something that must be done to maintain good health.

The viral infection may be congenital or occur through infection from an already infected vampirist. In some individuals, the virus never breaks out even though they are carrier of it. It also happens that the body's immune system can fight off the virus before the carrier reaches puberty, resulting in vampirism not emerging. Whether of not the virus breaks out, infected children grow up and feel different to others, a sense of exclusion that is difficult to put words to. The HERV virus is also a selective virus, which means that it is not passed on to all offspring. If one of the parents is infected, there is a 25 percent chance that the child will be infected. If both parents carry the virus, the possibility increases to 50 percent.

The awakening look different depending on wheteher the afflicted has inherited the virus or been infected later in life. Congenital vampirism means a more gentle and slow transformation process, while those infected later in life undergo a drastic awakening over the span of a few days. This can mean pain and ailments. If the virus in congenital, awakening is often associated with puberty, because the virus is latent in the body and becomes active in response to increased hormone production.

The virus acts by integrating with the carrier's DNA, thus affecting the cellular structure. It also causes an overactivity in the sympathetic nervous system, which means that the body is in constant mild fight or flight state. This can be an unpleasant experience, as it means constant hyperactivity and restlessness during the first time with the condition. In most cases, the parasympathetic nervous system regulates the sympathetic by having a calming effect, but the HERV virus eliminates this function.

The constantly active nervous system brings about a lower body temperature, which explains the heat sensitivity of the vampirist. The blood is also drawn out from organs such as the skin, which both creates a pale skin and a sense of cold sweats. The constantly elevated adrenaline level also explains the increased strength of the vampirist. As the impulses to the brain increase in speed, fast reflexes and an ability to think faster are also obtained. One disadvantage is that the stress level in the body increases, which means they may need to develop methods that calms the body and mind.

Two infected vampirists can mutate the virus by drinking each other's blood. Through the blood exchange, the virus gets renewed and the vampiric abilities are further strengthened. The process is usually referred to as a superinfection. It is also a method that may be useful in cases where the virus has not reached the full potential of the carrier. When a vampirist passes on the virus, the process does not always succeed, the infected can then miss the positive effects and only suffer from anemia.

In a scientific article by Rebecca Hyman, professor at Oglethorpe University, the doctors Paul Cheney and Daniel Peterson hypothesized that there was a retrovirus similar to HIV, which affected the immune system negatively. They performed a series of tests on sample patients who showed symptoms such as extreme fatigue, insomnia, impaired memory and dizziness. The investigations did not yield any answers as to what caused the symptoms, but as the doctors were convinced that a retrovirus was the basis of the problem, the results were sent for further analysis to the *Centers for Disease Control* (CDC) in Atlanta. However, CDC did not find anything, so the hypothesis could be written off.

The symptoms that the physicians witnessed and their hypothesis about the cause are similar to the HERV virus theory. It is therefore not an unreasonable assumption that it may have its basis in Cheney and Peterson's investigations. What the advocates seem to have missed is that the theory could never be confirmed and that there is no scientific basis for the claim. The advocates, on the other hand, claim that the HERV virus theory is the only one that is scientifically sustainable and that it can be proven – but that only a little more research is needed in the field.

Some also refer to a specific gene that researches found can double the lifespan of fruit flies, which is said to give credibility to the HERV theory. Researchers have discovered that if the gene is being manipulated, it increases the life span. In theory, this could create immortality. Some vampirists claim that they have undergone this type of cellular change for a long time, but that the phenomenon has not been observed by the research community.

Although there is currently no research to present that supports the HERV theory in its entirety, it is the most advanced in the vampirist world. Scientific explanations that are completely or partially lacking any basis in observable reality are commonly referred to as pseudoscience. By dressing their arguments up, it may seem that the theory is more well-founded than it actually is. In an effort to create credibility for a pseudoscientific theory, real research results can be distorted, and they are often transferred to environments that do not in any way correspond to the condition of the original study. In this way the advocates can create far-fetched explanatory models for integrating research into their own theory.

Chapter 6

Blood Drinking Vampirists

'The blood is the life … and it shall be mine!'

(From the movie *Bram Stoker's Dracula*, 1992)

THE BODY FLUID that is primarily associated with vampirism is the blood. Some also say that only the blood drinking vampirists are the real thing. But how do they get the coveted blood? And maybe the most important question of all of them, from where? I imagine what most people envision is a mysterious pale figure in a cloak that sinks their sharp teeth down in the victim's bare throat, leaving behind fang marks. However, this is a procedure that many vampirists advice against, as it is associated with too many risks.

The Importance of Blood and Medicine

Blood is a symbol of life, without the blood being pumped around in our veins, we would be empty shells – dead. The idea that someone is looking for what keeps your body alive can be frightening. It is therefore not very strange if we get upset when someone expresses this desire. However, humans are used to being at the top of the food chain. Being suddenly reduced to prey means an uncomfortable change of power.

Blood has played an important role in medical history. According to Indian Ayurvedic Medicine, which dates back to 1200-900 BC, the human body consists of seven parts: plasma, blood, meat, fat, bone, marrow and semen. Antique Greeks were inspired and believed that the body consisted of four fluids: blood (air), phlegm (water), yellow bile (fire) and black bile (earth).

All medical treatment was based on maintaining or achieving a balance between the fluids. The body was considered self-healing and exercise, rest and proper food could cure most illnesses. But if it did not produce the desired results, bloodletting could become applicable. The idea behind bloodletting was to empty the body on some of the fluids, thus eliminating the sickness. Some diseases were also thought to be due to an abundance of blood and the excess was rotting in the body. Occasionally, the patient lost too much blood, so many deaths can result from this method. It was not only sick people who were let of blood, but it was considered a healthy cleansing process that could be done occasionally. Another popular method was cupping. By cupping, the liquids could be pulled out with the help of vacuum. A somewhat brutal method was trepanation, which is when a hole is drilled in the patient's skull.

It was not always about emptying the patient on blood. A popular method of curing everything from whooping cough to epilepsy was drinking blood.

Although blood had long been regarded as an important part of medical art, it was only during the 17th century that we discovered that the blood is pumped around the body. The practice of the four liquids was abandoned as late as during the 19th century and was replaced by modern medical theory.

Blood Thirsty Vampirists

A common misconception is that the vampirist feeds exclusively on blood. The truth is that their bodies require a varied and nutritious diet. Unlike ordinary people, they complement the dietery circle with blood. However, it is not uncommon with claims about different types of food allergies, some also say that they have a higher tolerance to alcohol.

The most controversial question when it comes to the subject of bloodthirsty vampirists, is their drinking habits. There are many different opinions regarding how often blood drinking should occur. Some say they need blood every week, while for others it is enough once a month. There are even cases where the vampirist claims that drinking blood only once every five years is enough. When it comes to quantity, it is also very different. Some vampirists manage with only a few drops, while others drink a few table spoon fulls or more. It is therefore clear that there exists a large variation in both quantity and frequency.

What happens if the vampirist does not get enough blood? Many testify that they feel weak and more irritable. The symptoms of vampirism are also becoming more apparent, for example, sensitivity to light can be exacerbated. Drinking blood brinds a feeling of calm and an almost euphoric feeling, some say it resembles a rush.

How come some vampirists experience a desire for blood? Essentially, there are two camps on the issue; Those who consider it to be due to energy shortages and those who consider it to be a lack of blood (anemia). Those who advocate the theory of anemia suggest that their organs, such as heart and brain, require a greater amount than normal to function. A result of the deficiency is the perceived paleness, as there is simply not enough blood. Drinking blood then becomes a way to compensate for the deficit. The second view is that blood drinking is about stored energy. The blood that has been pulsed in the donor's body is considered very powerful and because of it, it is preferable to drink directly from the source.

Another common notion is the idea that blood consumption connects people through the action, and that the vampirist literally creeps under the skin of the donor. That someone is willing to sacrifice his blood can give a sense of power and invincibility. Whether it is about taking on lost blood or blood energy, both camps agree that the vampirist body is not capable of producing it on its own – an external source is required.

Human Donors

Blood drinking requires that someone supplies the vampirist with blood. When the subject of blood is spoken, grotesque scenes containing tyranny, barbaric methods or even manslaughter comes to mind. However, the inhabitants of the vampirist community care for their already ragged reputation and distance themselves from such actions.

In order to gain access to blood without force or violence, willing blood donors are required. These people are usually called donors, but some prefer epithets as sources or victims. However, with the vampirists there is a strong resistance to call donors this, meaning they should be treated with respect. They are, after all, the ones that allows the vampirist to quench her bloodthirst. Nor would it be fruitful to kill or damage its donor, as it is in their interest to maintain a steady and lasting blood source.

Blood is associated with life because it is something we need to live. The blood thus has an inherent force. According to this reasoning, blood drinking can be seen as a ritual where the vampirist enjoys the vitality from the donor. It's not just 'ordinary' people who can become donors, this possibility exists for vampirists too.

The perceptions differ as to how the relationship between vampirist and donor can and should look. Some declare that human beings and vampirists should live separately, and that the relationship should not therefore be developed into a friendship or love relationship. The position is based on the assumption that 'one does not play with the food' as well as the abnormality of having a sexual relationship with another species. This group often also tends to see the vampirist as superior to human beings, thus considering their donors as nothing but food. Thankfully, this view seems to have a relatively limited spread. Vampirists often develop a protective relationship with their donor instead.

Their motives fit together like puzzle pieces. The donor has a deep wish to be desired and seen. The vampirist, on the other hand, often appreciates the sense of power that comes to mind when someone is prepared to sacrifice his blood, his vitality, to this. At first glance donors may seem to be the ones who sacrifice the most in the relationship, but they seem to get at least as much out of their role.

The vampirist is advised to choose her donor with care. It is important that the donor is fully healthy, both in terms of physical and mental health. The more facetious vampirists claim that people with emotional personality disorder and self-harm tendencies are appropriate candidates, referring to their tendency for cutting themselves and the attention that the donor role brings.

Apart from that, donors should be of legal age, given the legal consequences the procedure may otherwise bring. On the *Shadowlore* website (no longer available) there is even a donor database. There, vampirists and donors can list their e-mail addresses, distributed by hometown. Everyone on the site must be at least 18 years old.

A strong recommendation is that the vampirist and donor establish a joint contract setting out the conditions for cooperation. For example, the contract may indicate that the donor must test for various diseases and with what continuity it will take place. The contrakt can also indicate how often, and by what method, the donor is expected to provide blood and/or energy. It should be stated which rights the donor holds and what is required to break the contract. Many vampirists recommend that the contract states that the donor is free to terminate the cooperation whenever he desires, especially if discomfort or something else would occur. It is important that the donor feels safe and that the vampirist respects when the donor says no. In cases where the vampirist bites her donor or prefers to drink the blood directly from the donor's body, it is also important that the vampirist constantly tests for diseases, something that should also be noted in the contract.

Tools and Risks

Most vampirists do not bite their donor. Biting is considered unhygienic, dangerous and ineffective. In addition, there is a high risk of damage, infection and scarring. It is painful and there are also easier ways to access the blood. But if biting does not belong to the repertoire, how will the vampirist get access to the blood?

Common tools to use are different types of needles and knives. Of course, it is not harmless to cut into people's bodies or to drink their blood. By using sterile tools and regularly testing for bloodborne diseases, the risks of blood extraction can be minimized.

Lansets, which are usually intended for diabetics, are a popular method. It is a relatively safe method with minimal risk of scarring. The downside is that there is only a small amount of blood that can be obtained at a time, but many vampirists say it's enough.

For those who want larger blood volume or like the sight of flowing blood, razor blades or scalpels are an option. For hygienic reasons, it is important that the blade is sterile and that it is only used once. As the method can provide a greater amount of blood, it also means increased risk taking. It's incredibly easy to accidentally puncture an artery or to cut too deep. An open wound, on the other hand, always means an infection risk, however small it is. Cutting up the skin with a tool also means a risk of scarring. Beginners often cut too deeply, so it may be good practice, for example, on an orange first. You do not need to see blood immediately, but the advise is to wait for a few seconds to allow the skin to open. The donation also means that a major responsibility lies with the vampirist. For example, it is important to keep in mind that the amount of blood lost is not getting too great and that the donor does not start to feel ill.

When a cannula is used, it is easier to keep track of the amount of blood donated. Since there i also a smaller skin area that i punctured, the risk of scarring is not as great.

Regardless of the method used, it is important to always wear gloves. The skin should also be washed with antibacterial soap and lubricated with antiseptic lotion and/or alcohol. The wounds must also be washed and bandaged after the donation is complete.

Different Types of Human Blood

Gourmet vampirists recognize differences between blood, even though all varieties come from humans. Some believe that the best blood comes from other vampirists, and that such a blood exchange can even further enhance the vampiric abilities (so-called superinfection). Stereotypically enough, blood from virgins is also hailed as extremely clean and tasty. Some also find that different blood types have different quality and taste. It is relatively common to prefer a blood that has not been aired. This may be the reason why some vampirists drink the blood directly from a syringe, for example.

The blood should preferably be warm, and ingestion should take place immediately. However, if a cutting tool is used, the blood may cool down. But how the blood is consumed is not just about temperature. For some vampirists, it is also a matter of nutritional content. Blood fed directly from the donor's body, for example from an open wound, is considered to be more energy rich. These vampirists claim that a larger amount of blood is required if a cannula is used than in direct consumption. They say that it is the donor's energy they want and that by removing the psychical contact, the amount of energy is also reduced. This perception often goes hand in hand with the belief that all vampirists really suffer from energy deficiency – and that the blood is a useful medium to replenish the reserves. In physical contact with the donor, the vampirist then receives energy from both blood and life force.

An alternative is also to drink their own blood. To compulsively drink one's own blood is called autovampirism. Psychiatrist Philip D. Jaffé and Professor Frank DiCataldo argue that autovampirism should not be confused with self-harm of suicide attempts. In autovampirism, like other vampirism, the blood is the focus and the main purpose is to drink the blood. When self-harm happens, blood drinking may also occur, but the primary reason for the action is usually described as a form of emotional management.

Some believe that the illness anemia can contribute to a thirst for blood, probably because of the body's lack of it. A scientific article by Halevy, Levi, Shnaker and Orda states that blood drinking resulting from anemia is very rare, but that a possible cause of the illness can be autovampirism itself. The article present a case where an anemic patient cut herself repeatedly to consume blood. The blood that the patient swallowed was collected in the stomach and the blood loss resulting from the self-injury was judged to be the cause of the patient's anemic condition. The authors highlight the importance of attention from healthcare professionals, especially regarding recurring patients.

Strangely enough, it seems unusual to drink menstrual blood. It is, after all, a very accessible alternative and, moreover, one that does not involve bloody risk-taking in the form of punctured arteries. It seems to be an impossible task to find a single vampirist who claims to drink it, even in cases where the vampirist drinks her own blood. Perhaps it may be linked to the shame that exists today about the subject. Mentrual blood is still something that menstrualists worldwide learn to hide and not talk about. In view of this, it is unfortunately no wonder at all that this blood source seems to be forgotten even within the vampirist community.

Animalistic Alternatives

If the donor is out of town or for some other reason cannot supply the vampirist with blood, the thirst can be sated with animal blood. There are divided opinions whether animal blood is really a good alternative or not, but most still seem to advocate it. Animal blood is an easily accessible substitute, but its consumption depends on how picky the vampirist is. Some say, however, that is only helps temporarily and cannot completely replace human blood. A major advantage of animal meat is that, if properly cooked, it reduces the risk of suffering from diseases after consuming it. For the one who can handle it, organs like heart and liver are rich in blood and excellent food for the thirsty. Most people prefer warm, fresh blood and prefer to not choose frozen meat.

For those who choose animal source for their blood consumption, there are also different tastes preferences. Lamb is the blood that, to the greatest extent, resembles human blood to taste, although it has a slightly milder taste. Chicken is strongly advised not to consume, because the risk of disease is very real. The meat should be served as rare as possible, but depending on the meat type, it varies the amount of cooking required for the meat to be consumed without risk. If the vampirist is gastronomically gifted there are a variety of recipes with animal blood as an ingredient, such as blood pancakes and blood bread or why not a classic steak tartare?

The disadvantage of animal blood, as many claim, is that a larger amount needs to be consumed to achieve the same effect and still the desire. However, this is a price some vampirists are willing to pay due to the fact that it, compared with human blood, is safer to drink. Also, it is often easier to get hold of it.

Other Blood Substitutes

In the case of other blood substitutes, the subject is surrounded by major controversy. Some argue that foods as yogurt, fruit, vegetables, chocolate, red wine and ketchup can replace blood, a statement that is ridiculed and dismissed by those who think they know better. However, it is unusual to advocate such substitutes instead of the genuine product, but it is something that works in crisis situations. To many, it seems that it is about convincing yourself that it is blood, which results in the desire to be temporarily sated.

Other things that can take away the thoughts of the thirst are activities such as meditation or jogging. Other substitutes to temporarily help may be reddish beverages or lightly cooked meat, as it has a psychosomatic effect. This could be compared to the nicotine substitutes available – for example, the nicotine patches that can relieve the withdrawal for a smoker.

Iron Poisoning

So, a vampirists eating and drinking habits are made up mostly of the ordinary dietary circle. That only blood would be on the menu is considered a representation of fiction. Most people think that the vampirist is mostly a human being and that this requires the need for plain food. The vampirists who find themselves in need of blood are mostly using voluntary donors. However, drinking another person's blood is not risk free and it is not recommended. There is a risk of bloodborne diseases and may result in vomiting if the amount of blood consumed becomes too great. The vomiting is due to iron poisoning.

Some argue that the vampirist is immune to common diseases and therefore cannot be affected by these, which should, however, be taken with a grain of salt. Those who advocate the vampirist's blood drinking claim that the stomach acid is destroying the virus before it takes hold. However, if the vampirist has sores in her mouth there is a greater risk, because the route through the intestinal tract is bypassed and enters the bloodstream directly. Another common argument is that the vampirists body has developed a higher iron tolerance to enable blood drinking. However, it is common for those who experience a need to drink blood advocating a minimal consumption because of the risks of unwelcome side effects.

Another issue that matters here is what norms govern what we think is okay to eat and not. Is it the blood consumption that rubs us the wrong way, or is it consumption or our own species?

Many people today who do not identify themselves as vampirists receive blood daily through their meat consumption, especially if rare meat is the preference. But even here we make a difference. When you go to a restaurant you can probably order a steak tartare without raising any eyebrows, but if you would ask for a well-done dog steak you would have difficulty having your wishes met.

So, we perceive a difference between types of meat, but what about the blood? Let's say that any person on voluntary basis donates blood for you to drink, or alternatively that you drink animal blood. The animal has not voluntarily sacrificed its blood to you, but the human has. Which is the most ethically correct to consume?

Consuming body fluids of our own species is easily associated with anthropophagy, that is, cannibalism. Those who do not wish to stretch the limits can choose to live on animal blood, alternatively suppress their needs completely. Here, the psychic vampirists, those who feed on energy instead of blood, have a great advantage.

Blood Fetishism and Vampirism

Drinking blood, or feeling a desire for it, is not exclusive to vampirists. Human sexuality, and what turns us on, is complex. We all have different preferences, although in some cases normative structures can suppress our own desires. But, a sexual preference towards blood itself does not make the person in question a vampirist.

A crucial difference between blood fetishists and vampirists is the reason for blood consumption. For the fetishist it is erotic, while the vampirist needs the blood to restore some form of balance in the body. Of course, there are also different opinions about what applies. For example, some research shows that vampirism includes sexual excitement. However, for many vampirists, they have a need to supply blood to the body for survival, or at least for not getting sick.

Blood fetishism has a close relationship with BDSM, which does not necessarily mean vampirism does. There are, however, some similarities that are worth considering. For both BDSM practitioners and vampirists, it is about consenting individuals who, in some cases, can engage in blood games. Power and submission are also key components of both subcultures. Such a relationship becomes clear, for example, in the relationship between vampirist and donor.

Both subcultures are also considered as deviating from the norm and those we see as 'abnormal' tend to get a negative stamp. Individuals who engage in BDSM are often thought to have low self-esteem, mental health issues or have been exposed to social ills in childhood. However, such reasoning lacks research support. A scientific article from 2013 by DJ Williams summarizes previous research in the field. The overall conclusion from the studies is that there is no significant relationship. On the contrary, some studies have shown that BDSM practitioners have a better mental health in comparison to the non-subculture group. A number of studies also show that BDSM may have a therapeutic effect.

Chapter 7

Psychic Vampirists

'It looks dead. It smells dead. Yet it's moving around. That's interesting.'

(From the TV-series *Buffy the Vampire Slayer*, 1997-2003)

SO FAR, the book has primarily examined the blood drinking form of vampirism. In this chapter, I will examine vampirists who feed on energy – whether the energy is said to come from blood or other external sources.

Energy Fields and Healing

The psychic vampirists claim that the energy they absorb is a form of life force. The energy becomes something physical; an invisible substance that can be extracted from humans and nature through thought. In New Age, similar ideas about energy are common. The British documentary Three Miles North of Molkom from 2008 depicts a New Age festival at Ängsbacka conference center in Sweden. The festival is called No Mind Festival and offers a variety of workshops for its participants. Tree hugging, sweat lodge and tantric sex are some of the items on the program. The documentary also shows a kind of self-defence training. The exercise is to defend against physical attacks using mental energy. Through the right focus, the participant will learn the ability to create av impenetrable energy shield around her.

When mental energy is brought up, healing also comes to mind. Healing can be described as a way of channeling energy. A common method is to use your hands for the channeling. The purpose of healing is to heal or to make something whole and it is said to be a cure for most illnesses. An important part is that he who is being healed also wants to recover, it is not possible to force your healing power upon someone who is unwilling.

Vampirists Thirsty for Energy

Vampirism can sometimes be used as a negative taunt; people who seem to suck the energy out of you – you feel drained after just a short while. Psychic vampirists distance themselves from that kind of psychological vampirism and think what they are doing is something completely different. They claim that psychic vampirism may serve as a form of healing for the donor. From their point of view, psychological vampirism is instead about people with serious personality disorders who feed on other people's emotional energy.

A large part of the vampirist subculture claims that they are psychic vampirists. However, it is common for the blood advocates to reject the idea and state that there is no scientific evidence of psychic vampirism. They think it's a way for non-vampirists to claim their vampiric existence, because no-one can see the energy they say absorb. There are also those who go one step further and declare that those who believe in mental vampirism are simply brainwashed. According to this approach, the concept of mental vampirism only serves as an invitation to include as many people as possible in the vampirist community.

There seems to be a constant struggle between two camps: mental and blood drinking vampirists. However, energy advocates are not let down by this. Those who engage in the discussion retort and refer to the fact that blood consumption is primitive and only leads to iron poisoning. On the other hand, they often acknowledge blood as one of many sources of energy. As both groups get energy from another organism, some posit that they should both be counted as vampirists. The psychic vampirists get their energy through so-called life force, while the blood drinking vampirists get energy through the blood.

Psychic vampirism is rather seen as a mental ability than a medical condition. A psychic vampirist simply must regularly and actively pull in external energy to maintain a good physical, mental, emotional and spiritual health. The energy deficiency can be remedied in many ways, because not only people are filled with life force – it is everywhere. The vampirist is said to lack the ability to generate energy on its own and cannot store accumulated energy. Another common explanation for the energy deficiency is that the vampirist burns energy faster than ordinary people.

Like those who claim to experience anemis, psychic vampirists also claim that they suffer negative consequences when energy is low. Many testify that feeling low, or even depressed, can result if they do not acquire a sufficient amount of energy. The declining mood also affects the immune system, which has consquences in form of diseases. However, there appears to be no testimony that claims that energy depletion will lead to a definitive death. Energy is thus not vital to the vampirist, but it certainly helps to raise the quality of life and the sense of well-being. Some simply seems to like the feeling of consuming energy, they are exhilarated by it, but there is no threat to their survival if they are forced to be without it.

Those readers who consume a steady amount of caffeine on a daily basis can certainly recognize themselves. Being without the addictive substance can result in increased annoyance and a general bad mood. The energy deficiency of the vampirist simply resembles the withdrawal symptoms that the addict experiences.

Donation of Life Force

So how is it done? A psychic vampirist can get energy at a distance or through touch, but the process itself is about the same. How often the vampirist needs to replenish her energy varies, it can range from once a weel to only once a month.

Some vampirists use so-called chakra points on the human body to take energy. The energy can then be inhaled, or alternatively be flooded in through the palms. Some vampirists also use the imagination and imagine that they use a straw to draw in energy.

When touched, the palms can then be perceived as hot and the heat spreads through the rest of the body. It also happens that the act generates a taste of blood in the mouth. Psychic vampirists say they can feel the donor's energy flow into their own body, the donation thus makes the energy something tangible and almost material. Exactly how the vampirist experiences the energy they absorb seems to be different from person to person. The experience may also differ depending on where or who the energy comes from. As mentioned earlier, there are also vampirists who drink who drink blood to alleviate the energy thirst.

The energy donor probably has a less risky existence than those donating blood. They do not need to think about blood borne diseases, infection risks or wounds that do not stop bleeding. The donor is said to be able to experience a lower energy level, but otherwise there are no major dangers.

Donors testify that they can feel how life force pulses out of their bodies, like an open wound. After receiving energy, the vampirist feels revitalized, while the donor may feel tired and exhausted. As the experience can be overwhelming, the donor is advised to sit or lie down.

Psychic vampirism, like the blood drinking variant, is regarded as an intimate act. It is important that the donor can trust that the vampirist does not take too much. A major responsibility therefore rests on the vampirist to constantly be aware of the donor's reactions and mood.

Some vampirists claim that they can focus their energy intake and only remove 'the evil' – as a form of reverse healing. They say they can heal others, like removing pain and diseases. Vampirists who practice this type of energy intake mean they are feeding on the person's negative energy, which means a relief for the donor.

People with excessive energy are also said to be good donors. Being freed of part of their energy can make them calmer.

Different Types of Energy

Where does the energy the psychic vampirist speaks of come from? There are many different types of sources to drink from. When it comes to humans, the energy is particularly complex. Human energy can originate in, for example, thought, feelings or pure life force. Some also mean that they can extract sexual energy. This can be done by engaging in sexual activities, but the vampirist can get it also by using her charm to induce erotic feelings in the chosen person. All do not accept the latter, and state that in such cases it would be about sexual addiction – not vampirism.

Many psychic vampirists seem to use a personal donor as they draw energy through different methods. But there are also other variants. Human energy can come from blood, because blood is also seen as a medium for energy. From this point of view, all vampirists are considered psychic, whether they drink blood or not. Some say, however, that this is a weaker form of vampirism and that the strongest vampirists manage to extract energy from humans in other ways. They do not need to go through the medium of blood, but rather through pure thought. There is also a category called 'hybrids' – they say they need both energy and blood.

Experienced vampirists can absorb energy several thousand kilometers away and do not even have to see the donor. The vampirists who claim to do something like this can thus use, for example, internet forums to gain energy. Some do prefer physical touch, wheteher they can absorb energy remotely or not. An intermediate variant is to absorb energy from larger crowds, which also ensures that too much energy is not taken from one and the same person.

Another branch in psychic vampirism concerns energy sources such as thunderstorms, running water and other phenomena outside the human body. All vampirists do not recognize this as a kind of vampirism, and state that it is only life force from people that can meet a vampirists needs. The vampirists who themselves use natural phenomena for their vitality claim that their vampirism is so powerful that they are not in need of human touch to extract energy.

It is probably easier for psychic vampirists than for the blood drinking one to meet her needs. That the life force should come from a human is something many seem to agree on, regardless if it is about blood or energy. Extracting energy from animal blood, yogurt or thunderstorms is viewed from this perspective as a weaker form of vampirism.

Unfortunately, other people can perceive the psychic vampirist as egocentric, attention-seeking and energy-draining. This is also a characteristic developed to create energy sources to 'drink' from, especially in cases where the vampirist is not aware of her situation. Indeed, by evoking a lot of emotion in others, for example through provocation, energy is released which the vampirist can then absorb. A satisfied vampirist has no reason for such behavior, which results in the personality being perceived as unstable and rapidly changing. This means it is important that the vampirist is aware of her nature. A vampirist with good self-awareness can control its energy intake and thus avoid intense emotional outbursts that harm people in her surroundings. Instead, the vampirist can consciously search for venues where much energy is released naturally – for example concerts or sporting events.

If the situation arises that the vampirist has no source of energy, then there are multiple substitutes available. Overall, it is energy-rich, and uplifting, food that is recommended. Everything from all kinds of fruits, energy drinks and peanut butter – yes, most things seem to work. Water is also sais to be a good source of extinguishing the thirst.

Psychosocial Aspects

In a case study conducted by Gubb, Segal, Khota and Dicks, published in *South African Psychiatry Review*, it appears that the concept of psychic vampirism refers to the act of consuming energy from an external source to strengthen one's own body. The researchers believe that psychic vampirism is about an energy intake that can be physiologically measured using the right technical equipment. Psychic vampirism can also be summarized as the act of absorbing energy from another human being.

The case study itself is about a man suffering from schizophrenia with psychotic and antisocial features.

He developed psychic vampirism, was conviced that he was a real vampire and said that he was in contact with other invisible vampires. He did not drink blood, but claimed that he could survive by 'zooming in' on other people. The researchers argue that the reason behind this behavior can be based on an attempt to connect with other people without the need for physical contact, which he had been struggling with since childhood.

In an other study, Neil Wilson has investigated psychic vampirism in relation to psychoanalytic treatment. The study was published in *The American Journal of Psychoanalysis* and included developmental psychological aspects that were linked to the idea of the vampire. The condition can occur if a person in childhood has grown up with a guardian who did not pay attention to the child's own needs, but instead mirrored himself in the child. The child gets used to receiving no respone from her environment and may have difficulty separating her own person from others. This could explain the experience of absorbing someone's energy, as the boundaries between the you and the self become fluid. The child mimics the caretaker's behavior and thus begins to use her surroundings for her own gain. Such an environment can also result in masochism, where the person is looking for a dominant life partner reminiscent of the guardian. The longing for togetherness is something that is common for most people. The vampirist is no exception.

PART III

Extremes

Chapter 8

Religious Vampirists

'What if there is no hell? Or they don't want us there? Ever think of that?'

(From the movie *Interview with the Vampire*, 1994)

THERE ARE A NUMBER of communities that represent different forms of vampirist religions, there are also satanists claiming to be vampirists. There are many who oppose this, rejecting the idea that vampirism automatically implies such life views. Some even claim that those who join any group, sect or other organization are not real vampirists. They assert that they do not belong to any group, and do best on their own. It is common for vampire-based religious groups to condemn blood drinking, while the general vampirist community generally tolerates it.

It is often very difficult to access information about the different religious societies. The information available is often what the groups themselves write on their website, and the membership is not rarely bound by an oath of confidentiality to disclose something for third parties.

New Age and Occultism

The word New Age originates from the 1960s and is difficult to define as it is a broad concept, but often refers to religious or spiritual communities formed recently.

In New Age movements, energy, reincarnation and life force are often spoken of, concepts originally derived from Eastern philosophy. Belief in spirits and the ability to communicate with the dead have been borrowed from spiritualism. In New Age, the spirits are often a kind of higher being that can provide guidance; a spiritual guide. Life in the physical body is seen as a temporary state that is taken advantage of by learning as much as possible, thus achieving a higher spiritual development. A major focus is, thus, on personal development.

In New Age, there is also a branch inspired by occultism, which can be described as an apocalyptic life view. Occultism in New Age means that a new age is coming and that it will be caused by one or more disasters.

Occultism really originates from the 16th century and has got its name from the Latin word for 'hidden'. It is usually included among the esoteric movements, although it is controversial. Esoterism focuses on spiritual development and has mysterious elements. A central theme is the belief that spiritual development leads to contact with higher beings. Many esoteric groups have some form of spiritual leaders who are responsible for educating the other members of the doctrine.

Vampiric Spiritual Communities

Occult groups represent a minority within the vampirist community, but as they have more resources available, they get more space than others. What they have in common is that they can be defined as new religious movements, though they do not always identify themselves as such.

Several vampirist organizations follow something called *The Black Veil*, which is an ethical code for vampirists. The first version was written by Father Sebastiaan, but it has since been revised on two occasions. Father Sebastiaan's version received much criticism as it was largely based on the roleplaying game *Vampire: The Masquerade*. Michelle Belanger oversaw the first rewriting, which aimed to make it more adapted to the reality of vampirists. The result of the first rewriting was that they increased the initial six articles to thirteen, and all references to the role-playing game were eliminated to increase credibility. However, in 2002, it was decided to rewrite its contents again. The latest version consists of seven articles consisting of moral and ethical guidelines that each vampirist should take into account. The language is now simplified and cleared from Gothic expressions that tend to be seen as deterring.

1. Discretion

Discretion is about being honest with ones vampiric nature, but not in such a way that other people will be frightened. The vampirist is urged to be cautious wiyh revealing herself to 'everything and everyone', and instead should tell people whom she trusts.

2. Diversity

Within the vampirist community, there are many different groups and world views. The vampirist is urged to have understanding and show respect for differing opinions. The point is that no teaching is the only correct one.

3. Control

This point refers to control of one's desires. The vampirist is reminded that the desire and the 'darkness' cannot take over. It's also important to never use vampiric powers to hurt others or be overpowering. The hunger is presented here more as a necessary evil than anything else.

4. Elders

Vampire group leaders should be respected, but not blindly so. The vampirist is urged to follow only those who deserve it. A good leader can show the way, but it is always up to the individual to follow in her footsteps or not.

5. Behavior

The vampirist must always think through her actions and always strive to not harm others. This also includes the ability to identify risks and avoid them. A catchphrase is to treat others as you would want them to treat you.

6. Donors

Only adults are considered suitable donors and there should always provide informed consent. The vampirist is also prompted to respect her donor and ensure that there is a reciprocity in the relationship between them.

<u>7. Community</u>

Finally, the vampirist is encouraged to seek out a community in the subculture to find similar people and exchange thought and questions. Being in a community also implies a responsibility for the individual. Criminal acts are distanced from, as such behavior results in the whole community being harmed.

House Kheperu

House Kheperu was founded by previously mentioned vampirists Michelle Belanger and Father Sebastiaan, however, only Belanger currently leads the group. Occasionally, meetings are held for the members. The purpose of the meetings is to spread information through various forms of workshops and lectures. They practice a spiritual form of vampirism that includes healing and shamanism.

They have adopted their name after an Egyptian word for change. By that, they refer to the development that takes place by practicing their vampiric abilities. Through more knowledge, they can reach a new level of awareness about themselves and the universe.

House Kheperu claim that they originate from ancient Egypt and that they have been reincarnating ever since. They think it's reincarnation that has developed their ability to handle energy. They themselves say they do not constitute a religion or view or life, and let each member 'seek their own truth'.

The movement uses a cast system where one belongs to one of the three casts: priest, warrior or counselor. They emphasize that this is not to be seen as a hierarchical order, everyone fulfills their function based on their own background and are therefore equally important. What cast a Kheprian belongs to depends on energy management. For example, the 'priests' require a lot of energy, while the 'warriors' have a lower energy consumption, but can instead provide protection against mental energy attacks. Finally, there's the intuitive and emotionally conscious 'counselor'. Everyone is free to independently identify which of the three casts one belongs to.

House Kheperu prefers the term Kheprian instead of vampirist or vampire. They say that a Kheprian not only parasitizes on their donors, but the donors also have something to gain by the arrangement. When the Kheprian absorbs energy, something happens in the donor's body that can be experienced as a sense of recovery. The easiest way to imagine this would be when the Kheprian absorbs negative emotions or uses healing. From this perspective, their vampirism is more about transformation and renewal than unilateral gain.

Ordo Sekhemu

Ordo Sekhemu was founded by Reverend Vicutus and the members call themselves Sekhrians. They are aimed at vampirists who have an interest in black magic and occultism – they also have their own creation story. However, they claim that it is a question of definition whether they are satanists or not. Their main argument is that each one is her own God and that their members are free to decide their life view. This means that it is fully possible to be, for example, Christian, and at the same time a Sekhrian. This is possible because they mean that their theology has united all the religions of the world.

They regard vampirism as a spiritual state and the leading word is spiritual development. They sacrifice neither humans nor animals, but blood can be sacrificed to spirits or used to make deals. The group otherwise practices psychic vampirism, but blood is considered a flow of energy, and blood drinking is used in conjunction with rituals. The blood is mixed on these occasions with wine.

It is not easy to become a member of the house. *Ordo Sekhemu* consists of three differens levels: the outer, the dedicated and the inner circle. The outer circle consists of not yet official members who aspire for membership. The devotees begin approaching a full membership and are dedicated to studying the sectarian world view with the support of a mentor. When the mentor thinks that the dedicated is ready, he or she may undergo an exam that puts their knowledge to the test. The inner circle consists of *Ordo Sekhemu's* official members and here there are different degrees to achieve depending on the individual's spiritual development. In addition, *Ordo* Sekhemu also uses a cast system similar to *House Kheperus*.

Countess Elizabeth Vampire Coven

Countess Elizabeth Vampire Coven (CEVC) was founded in England in 2003 by the vampirists Countess Elizabeth and Father Ruthven. They have openly acknowledged that they borrow a lot of their teachings from *House Kheperu* and *The Temple of the Vampire*. What separates the group from both of the above mentioned is that they engage in blood drinking vampirism, but they also welcome different forms of psychic vampirism. In fact, they regard vampirism as a consequence of energy deficiency, which means they see blood as a medium of life force.

Their faith revolves around black magic, occultism and rituals. The group believes that the rituals derive from *The Order of the Blood Adepti*, which is said to be a secret order that existed until 1876.

A membership fee i 15 pounds per month and for that sum, the member receives a piece of jewelry, a weekly letter, a t-shirt and invitations to the community's various events. In order to have access to the events, that are organized on a monthly basis, everyone is required to wear the special jewelry.

The society also has its own bible, the *Blood Bible*. Members must be at least 18 years old and answer a questionnaire with questions regarding the purpose of their desire and about their vampiric nature.

CEVC consists of thirteen different clans and which clan a member belongs to depends on her strenghts and weaknesses.

Two communities that have a more pronounced religious appearance are *The Order of the Vampyre* and *The Temple of the Vampire*. What they have in common i that they see the vampire as a metaphorical ideal and to transform into its image requires willpower and occult studies.

The Order of the Vampyre

It can be said that *The Order of the Vampyre* began its path in satanism, more accurately with the *Church of Satan* (CoS). CoS was founded in 1966 in San Francisco by Anton Szandor LaVey. The church became famous for its black conventions, which only its own members were allowed to attend. During the conventions, naken women posed as altars to symbolize the lusts of flesh, which is one of the church's central starting points. Despite the name, it is not the devil who is at the center, but rather it is an individualistic atheism focusing on self-realization.

In 1975, Lilith and Michael Aquino, then members of CoS, decided to break away and start their own order. The couple thought that CoS had become too commercial and had an unhealthy financial focus, so they created *The Temple of Set*. As expected, this refers to the Egyptian god Set, which is at the heart of the temple's beliefs. Individualism and self-realization are the focus of the members. Finally, *The Order of the Vampyre* was founded in *The Temple of Set* in 1984 and constitutes the orders vampire department.

One of the founders, Michael Aquino, claims that he has spiritual contact with the Egyptian god Set. According to him, they have communicated through automatic writing and the orders holy scriptures are the result of their conversation. In addition, Aquino believes that he is a reincarnation of Aleister Crowley (1875-1947), a progenitor of today's occultism.

The Order of the Vampyre is secretive, and their total membership count is unknown. Few are allowed entry because they are very selective. It is required that the applicant has a membership in *The Temple of Set* and that she has achieved a certain rank in it. The order advocates individualism and members communicate through newsletters – *Nightwing* and *The Vampire*

Papers. Physical meet-ups can occur, but they are rare – only once a year. Membership is not free and climbing the hierarchy requires the purchase of the orders literature and courses.

Self-realization and achieving your perfect potential is the basic starting point, the vampire constitutes only a metaphor for the powers and abilities a member can develop by studying the occult. They do not identify themselves av vampires and drinking blood is not allowed. The reason for the order's distancing of all forms of vampirism comes from LaVey's book *The Satanic Bible*. The book describes psychic vampires as demanding personalities that drain you of energy and emotions. As mentioned earlier, drinking blood is not allowed. For this reason, vampirists are not welcome in either *The Temple of Set* or in *The Order of the Vampyre*.

As self-realization is the main goal of *The Order of the Vampyre*, and a member achieves this, the member is then in a state called 'xeper', which means having self-awareness and to seeing your full potential. However, the order does not have a communal religious practice, but leave to each member to find their way. The members' goal is to become one with the vampiric essence, which for them is a sophisticated elegance. To do this, the member is dedicated to practicing her ability to visualize. Studies of art, music and literature are also encouraged.

The vampire also symbolize power, which is the key motivational factor in the order. In short, it is about the order teaching techniques to control the environment in the direction you want it to go. For a person who masters this ability, wealth, happiness – and eternal life, follows.

The Temple of the Vampire

The author Joseph Laycock means that *The Temple of the Vampire* is highly controversial and Arleno Russo writes in her book *Vampire Nation* from 2008 that the society is difficult to gain insight into as it is open to members only. The Temple was founded by George C. Smith, who also goes under other assumed names like Nemo or Lucas Martel. Their world view includes a totalitarian approach, meaning they believe that they are the only true vampire religion. *The Temple of the Vampire* holds legal status as a religion in the United States, which they have had since its inception in 1989.

An unconfirmed theory that flourished is that the *The Temple of the Vampire* originates from *Church of*

Satan (CoS), and that is was founded with the purpose to compete with *The Temple of Sets* vampiric department *The Order of the Vampyre*. The rumor probably is based on the fact that *The Temple of the Vampire* was founded just a few years after the Aquino's broke out of CoS to start *The Temple of Set*. In addition, the founder of *The Temple of the Vampire* (George C. Smith) is also a former member of CoS.

Blood drinking is condemned and is not accepted among its members. This is because of the society's fundamental belief that vampirists do not engage in such barbarism. Crime is also not accepted. The member may not be active in other organizations whose rules contrast with the Temples. It is also forbidden to discuss the Temple with third parties. Breaking any of the temple rules will result in immediate exclusion.

In their opinion, only their members are true vampirists. They base this claim on the view that is is only the Temple that can teach the true ability to absorb energy from its surroundings. *The Temple of the Vampire* are also elitist in its selection of members; Only people who are born vampirists are welcome.

There is no physical temple, as all communication and interaction take place on the internet. On the Temple's website, however, it is possible to read that their members-exclusive internet forum *Lifeforce* can serve as a tool for members to organize various gatherings themselves. According to a previous member, all correspondence happened through e-mail, so there were never any physical meetings. The person in question also said that he received the highest rank of the Temple only by purchasing their various products and paying the membership fee.

On the website you can apply for membership and purchase literature. Among other things, the company's own *The Vampire Bible*, that is an obligatory requirement to buy if you want membership, is sold. There are two different forms of membership; 'active' and 'passive'. Everyone is free to order a copy of *The Vampire Bible* for $60, and membership costs $20 per month. However, the monthly fee only means a 'passive' membership. On the whole, the passive membership can be regarded as an economic sponsorship of the Temple.

To gain more insight and have the opportunity to advance within the organization, an application for a so-called 'active' membership is required. To become an active member of the Temple, $75 is required in application fees and the aspirant needs to submit a copy of her ID to verify identity and age. They only accept members over the age of 18. As an active member, you gain access to the Temple's internet forum *Lifeforce*, a constantly updated PDF with information and discounted prices on the Temple's all products. To advance within the Temple hierarchy, the member must buy various products. The fact that the membership seems to depend on giving as much money as possible to the Temple, hopefully makes most people question it.

The Temple consists of two different parts, 'Dayside' and 'Nightside'. 'Dayside' includes those sections of religious practice that are open to those who are subscribed to active membership, including access to the locked internet forum. It is also through this part of the religion that the member can advance within the internal hierarchy. There are five different levels: 'initiate', 'predator', 'priest'/'priestess', 'sorcerer'/'sourceress' and 'adept'. The titles are obtained deending on how far your learning process has come – that is, how many of the books you have bought. In addition to the base book, *The Vampire Bible*, there are four more bibles: *The Vampire Predator Bible*, *The Vampire Priesthood Bible*, *The Vampire Sorcery Bible* and finally *The Vampire Adept Bible*. Each bible is linked to the respective titles of the organization.

'Nightside' includes the magic part of the religion. The literature describes the techniques the Temple teaches to achieve the greatest possible power. Through the practice of the religion the member can, for example, learn to control her dreams. Part of the exercise, of course, consists of psychic vampirism. The teaching of the Temple is based on the absorption of people's life force. Life force is only reserved for member of the Temple to absorb, as others do not have the knowledge or power to achieve this. The division between 'Dayside' and 'Nightside' is also based on the belief that everyone has both of these parts within them. 'Dayside' is the part of the self that is visible outwards, while 'Nightside' holds the more mysterious, vampiric and supernatural aspects.

They claim that they are a different kind of religion, as they do not worship or idolize any external higher power. Instead, they claim that their form of religious practice allows domination over death and other forces that are unavailable to third parties. Another claim is that is is the Temple that created all the religions of the world. The purpose of this has been to control as many people as possible.

The Temple means that it is only members of its community that are the ones who will survive the coming apocalypse. *The Vampire Bible* reveals that in the beginning, people had direct contact with the undead gods, who were idolized and received sacrificial gifts. The contact, however, was ruined, which has resulted in the undead gods regularly claiming their gifts. When it reaches its culmination, the gods will again take psysical form and descend on earth to rule. Through the practice of religion, the temple members have also developed the ability to become undead gods themselves after the death of the physical body. Thus, the members of the Temple will also become undead gods when the apocalypse comes, and the surviving people will serve as energy sources for the gods. With all the products members are expected to buy, it seems that the gods can be bribed with capitalist means.

The starting point is very similar to that found in satanism, that the individual is her own God. The Temple thus does not worship any higher power, but is instead based on each one's inherent power. They claim that their purpose is to teach their members how to achieve absolute autonomy. The teachings encourage members to embrace their animal instincts and the fact that they are a predator. They believe that magic exists, but there is neither heaven nor hell. Members are encouraged to take advantage of life here and now and to focus on getting the maximum possible profit from life. Nor is there any need for member to feel stressed as they think their teachings place them on a path to immortality.

According to the Temple, the vampire is a natural step in evolution. They thus also consider themselves superior to the ordinary person. A paradox is that they are strong advocates of individualism, personal freedom and reject the need for group affiliation. This at the same time as they are very clear that it is only their group members who are followers of the true vampire religion. The guiding principle is an independent life in which the practitioner through the community of the Temple can achieve good health, wealth and eternal life.

Sects and Closed Communities

Both *The Order of the Vampyre* and *The Temple of the Vampire* are apparently closed communities that outsiders have difficulty gaining insight into. Members are also called upon to discretion and to keep their teachings internal. In addition, the membership costs money – a cost that becomes more expensive the higher up in the rank the member wants to come. The latter is especially clear when it comes to

The Temple of the Vampire. The fact that the Temple also has legal status as a religion means it is exempted from taxation.

These types of movements are not entirely unusual and are found primarily in different forms of sects. A distinctive feature of these sects is that they have a charismatic leader whose wisdom is not allowed to be questioned.

A sect can also be difficult to leave. Sometimes it may be because the sect does not want internal knowledge to spread, while in other cases it is about the movement not allowing contact with 'fallen' members. Defectors sometimes risk being subjected to serious harassment, which makes it difficult to start a new life outside of the movement. Violence and threats of violence against pets, family and friends may occur. The fact that several sects prohibit contact with the outside world also have consequences. It is not uncommon for families to be formed within the sect, in such cases, leaving can break all ties with both partners and childen.

To join a sect often requires the person to break her entire social life outside of the sect. The reason for this may be that the sect claims to know the only truth. Everyone outside the sect is thus regarded as less knowledgeable and as destructive to the purity of the group.

To question the movement or its leaders is comparable to questioning God. Violation of the rules are punished by both physical and mental mens. It is common for the member not to get all the knowledge that the movement shares at once, but instead it is revealed gradually. With more knowledge, the member also climbs in the hierarchy. It is the leader who is seen as having full knowledge and the one who desides who is ready to receive the information, and when. That is, to move on in her development. In this way, a member is also compelled to stay.

An early example, whose structure has also inspired many of today's sects, is the *Illuminati Order*. The order was formed by Adam Weishaupt (1748-1830) in Germany and existed during the period 1776-1785. The movement wanted to achieve world domination, whose purpose was for the devil to take over later. Within the group there was a clear hierarchy, of which the leader was at the top and called himself 'king'. The order would attract highly educated people and thus became very elitist. As a new member, you started at the bottom and were considered ignorant. When the aspirant proved her worth to the leader, higher levels could be achieved, after which new knowledge followed – in this case, different codewords, information about the purpose of the order and who were members. Only those who were at the top of the inner circle had complete information. It was all set up as a form of course with different parts, which became increasingly difficult after each level. All communication between members happened in code and it was strictly forbidden to talk about the words with outsiders.

A modern example of a sect is the *Church of Scientology*. The church was originally founded in 1954 by L. Ron Hubbard (1911-1986) and is still today represented as a kind of superior man.

The structure is largely reminiscent of the *Illuminati Order*, as members of the church also climb a hierarchy with the help of the movement's education. The church markets itself as a movement that through religious philosophy aims at spiritual and personal development, the goal is to achieve total insight. Of course, it is only the church that can offer the services required to reach it. A large part of this journey is based on 'auditing', which can be described as a combination of counseling and confession.

For an outsider, life in a sect may feel extremely absent from reality and it can be hard to understand how a person can allow himself to be subjugated.

Programming takes place gradually and the normalization process follows. The member usually does not notice what has happendes until it is too late. It often happens to well-educated and intelligent people. On the other hand, it is common for people to be more receptive to the message of the sect, for example in the middle of a life crisis. It may seem that the sect comes with the answers that have been so long sought after.

As the sect strictly controls what information comes to the outside world, they can also manipulate the view of the movement, which can often be perceived as harmless from the outside.

Chapter 9

Vampirists Who Commit Murder

'Did they look like psychos? Is that what they looked like? They were vampires. Psychos do not explode when sunlight hits them, I don't give a fuck how crazy they are!'

(From the movie *From dusk till dawn*, 1996)

VAMPIRIC MURDERS HAVE always fascinated. It is hardly shocking that violent crimes with vampiric elements are shown in news media as bestial acts committed by a murderous maniac who believes himself to be a vampire. In many cases, the criminal gets the epithet 'vampire' by the media. An example of this is Francois Bertrand, who is notorious for his necrophilia during the 1840s. Francois dug up dead bodies and had sex with them. He was one of the first criminal who was referred to as a 'vampire', despite his purely necrophilic acts. There is nothing that proves that Francois Bertrand thought of himself as a vampirist and he probably would not have been called that if he was of an earlier generation.

Behind the headlines, it is usually people who suffer from some form of mental illness and do not themselves identify themselves as vampirists. That crimes of this kind are associated with the vampirist community are a major problem for today's 'real' vampirists, since they do not want to be associated with such behavior.

Where the line is drawn is also a question of definition, because what truly is a vampirist? Should necrophilia, as Herschel Prins means, also be included? Before I begin, I would like to make it clear that this is not a complete account of killers who claim to be vampirists, it is only a selection of the ones I personally find most interesting. The amount of vampire related movies and books has exploded and with it, the tendency to identify as one has also increased.

There are gender differences in how we interpret the motives and personal qualities of serial killers. Male coded killers tend to more often be associated with the vampire's alleged charisma and charm. For this group, the violent crime also becomes something that further reinforces male gender identity. The act is seen as morally wrong, but power, violence and dominance are stereotypical features attributed to the male role. This results in the interpretation of the behavior as hypermasculinity – it has assumed abnormal proportions. Female coded killers are instead perceived as unfeminine and the violence is a sign that they failed to live up to their gender role. It becomes a conflict of roles, as we cannot as easily incorporate the actions into our social construct of what it means to be a woman. The focus is, therefore, rather to defeminize the actions, rather than joining it with vampirism.

Possibly this may be part of the explanation for the overrepresentation of men who commit so-called vampire murders – and thus the gender distribution in this chapter. The sexual orientation is also more often spoken of when it comes to female coded killers. They are often referred to as lesbians and are often accused of hating men; something that rarely happens to the male counterpart even though their victims are often, women.

As with other people, however, regardless of gender, it is very unusual and rare that a vampirist commits murder. Many of the portrayed cases in this chapter have had other diagnoses, but regardless of diagnosis, they belong to a minority of the afflicted. Vampirists can commit murder, but it is not a significant symptom of the condition. Vampire murders are headline material and attract much attention, which results in the vampire image being misleading.

DJ Williams, professor at Idaho State University, believes that most individuals within the group live normal and healthy lives. According to Williams, vampirism should be seen as a form of personal expression and not automatically linked with neither crime nor mental illness.

Peter Kürten (1883-1931, Germany)

Peter Kürten, 'The Vampire from Düsseldorf', did not identify himself as a vampirist, but he stated that he was sexually excited by blood. Before Peter started to assault people, he engaged in bestiality with sheep. It seems to have been blood drinking, necrophilia and rape that attracted him. In light of his actions, he should primarily be considered a sex murderer.

In 1913 a 10-year-old girl with two wounds on her throat was found, she also had severe injuries to the genitals. A total of 16 years later, an 8-year-old girl and a 45-year-old man were found in a short span of time; both dead. The man had been stabbed over twenty times, of which several blows were to the temple.

A few months later, two girls, aged 5 and 14 were found strangled to death. The older girl's head was removed from the body. More and more bodies were found, but there was no suspects.

One day a letter was sent to the police with instructions for were two missing girls were. The letter was written by a Peter Kürten and when the police found the girls, they were both dead.

When Peter was arrested, he pled guilty to 13 murders and several other assaults. He also told that he had drunk blood from several of the victims. Peter Kürten was executed on July 2, 1931.

Fritz Haarmann (1879-1925, Germany)

Fritz Haarmann was a pedophile, serial killer and cannibal who supposedly killed about 24 young men. He is called 'The Vampire from Hannover', which comes from that he is believed to have drank of his victim's blood. The bodies were butchered, and Fritz then sold the meat in the local food market.

Already at the age of 17, he was arrested for pedophilia and was sent to a psychiatric clinic. He escaped and returned to a life of crime. Fritz was often caught for his crimes and spent much of his life behind bars.

Finally, he was found guilty for several murders and received death penalty. Fritz himself wished to be beheaded, and in 1925 his wish was fulfilled.

Bela Kiss (1877 – date of death unknown, Hungary)

In 1912 Bela Kiss married the fifteen-year younger Maria. Shortly after their marriage, Maria started a romance with a younger man. Around the same time, several women disappeared without a trace in his hometown, including Bela's wife.

Bela claimed that his wife traveled abroad with her new boyfriend. Bela shortly after enlisted in the army. While he was away, the landlord came to the house to check that it was in good condition. During the search, several bodies of women were found in alcohol-filled barrels. One of the was Maria. All victims had been strangled to death and emptied of blood. The number of barrels found varies depending on source, but it seems to have been between 20 and 30.

Bela Kiss was never convicted of his crimes. Before the horrendous evidence had surfaced, he had enlisted in the army and was probably killed in battle. His death could not be confirmed because the body was never found.

John George Haigh (1909 - 1949, England)

John George Haigh is perhaps most famous as the 'Acid Bath Murderer' or 'The Vampire of London' – nicknames he received because of his infamous approach.

John's deeds were motivated by his thirst for blood; a thirst that started early in his life. At the age of six, John began to injure himself so that he could lick the wounds. However, if he really drank his victims blood is unknown, as it could have been a strategy to avoid the death penalty.

John spent much time of his life in prison, mainly for minor crimes, such as fraud and theft. It is said that is was during his imprisonment that he started experimenting with acid and it was not long before he began to imagine what effect it would have on a human body. Using dead mice, he tried to figure out how long it would take for the acid to break down a whole human cadaver.

The murders were committed between September 1944 and February 1949 by John cutting his victims throats and drinking their blood. In a storage room he then kept barrels filled with sulfuric acid, in which he then kept the dead bodies. The purpose of the acid was to dissolve matter inside the barrels – that is the bodies of the victims. Often it did not take more than a few days before the body was fully dissolved, but in cases where the acid failed to fulfill its task, the body was cut into smaller pieces.

Nine people fell victim to John George Haigh before he was finally executed on August 10, 1949. Six of the dead were friends of the killer, while the remaining three appeared to be strangers.

Tracey Wigginton (1965 - , Australia)

One late night in 1989 Tracey Wigginton cut the throat of a man to drink his blood. She was not alone, as she did the deed with her friends. Tracey did not call herself a vampire, but got the label because of what was alleged during the trial. Her accomplices believed that Tracey had contact with Satan and that she had manipulated them with the aid of magic.

Richard Trenton Chase (1950 - 1980, USA)

Richard Trenton Chase is another of many violent criminals who got the name 'Dracula', but he is also known as 'The Vampire from Sacramento'. He drank the blood of his human and animal victims because he claimed to need it to survive. He was clearly disillusioned and a hypochondriac and was later diagnosed with schizophrenia due to his somatic delusions.

Richard's murder career began with a random shooting that took place in December 1977. The victim, 51-year-old Ambrose Griffin, died due to the injuries. It would, however, take a while before Richard was linked to the investigation, because the police did not know that the events were linked to each other.

On January 11, 1978, his neighbor reported that she saw him coming home with new pets regularly. Pets were not allowed in the apartment, and when the woman never saw the animals again she wondered what had happened to them.

On January 23 of the same year, a woman, Jeanne Laytom, reported that an unknown and unkempt man seemed to be spying on her house. It turned out later that Layton was mistaken, and it was the neighbors, the Edwards who were spied on. The Edwards couple had been on a day trip and when they returned home later that day, they found both urine and stool in their home.

A few hours later, the first human victim died. A 22-year-old named Teresa Wallin was attacked in her home. The perpetrator had shot her to death and then assaulted the body further; a nipple was cut off and the internal organs were exposed. Around the body, round marks were scrawled on the floor. The marks were of the victim's blood and the shape of the marks suggested that someone had placed a cup on the floor.

A few days later, January 27, 1978, another three people were found dead: two adults and one six-year-old child. The murdered man had been shot and the woman had been brutally stabbed. Her right eye as well as the liver were partially removed. Again, circular patterns were found on the floor. Shortly after the discovery, it was found out that the family had been babysitting a 22-month-old baby that day, but the child was nowhere to be found.

Following tip-offs from the public, suspicions turned to Richard and the police decided to visit his home. After some turbulence he was arrested and taken to the police station. The property was searched, but no trace of the 22-month-old baby was found. The apartment was very dirty, and blood was found everwhere – including in a drinking glass.

In the first hearing, Richard only acknowledged that he killed some dogs in his apartment, nothing else. The police, thus, had no confession at this time, but they had suspicions and Richard was arrested.

On February 16, 1978, it was reported from detention that Richard had admitted the murders to another inmate. Richard had told him that he drank the victim's blood because he suffered from blood poisoning. From the beginning he had only been drinking blood of animals but had tired of it and transitioned to humans instead. Richard also revealed that his choice of victims was highly random – he simply moved around in an area and entered randomly selected houses on his quest for blood. In true vampire fashion, he chose only unlocked houses, which he interpreted following an invitation. As for the 22-month-old baby, he had shot it to avoid noise. At home in the apartment he had drunk the child's blood. Afterwards, he had thrown the body in the garbage.

On March 24, 1978, the body of the 22-month-old was found behind a church. The body was found in a cardboard box, with the head laying under the body.

Richard Trenton Chase was sentenced to death. He died in 1980 after an overdose in prison.

Sean Richard Sellers (1969 - 1999, USA)

Sean Richard Sellers stood out as a child. He had a habit of bringing small bottles filled with blood to school, which he drank in front of his classmates. He read LaVeys The Satanic Bible and devoted much time to special rituals where he claimed to be communicating with the devil by writing messages with his own blood. Sean managed to find like-minded people and together they deepened their interest and began to drink each other's blood.

In September 1985 he shot and killed a shop assistant and shortly afterwards, he also murdered his parents.

Sean received the death penalty for his deeds.

Diana Semenuha (1976- , Ukraina)

Diana Semenuha was arrested in March 2005 after the discovery that she tricked homeless children into her home with the purpose of drinking their blood. To make the childen conform, she offered them a place to sleep, alcohol and glue to sniff.

Semenuha claimed that she needed the blood of the children to cope with a muscle disease. When the police raided her home, they found seven drugged children. She didn't claim to be a vampire, but a witch who was interested in the occult.

Tiffany Sutton (date of birth unknown, USA)

Tiffany Sutton had made plans to meet Robert McDaniel on Valentine's Day 2007. They most likely didn't know each other very well, but they were both interested in BDSM and had met on a forum for like-minded people. McDaniel volunteered to be bound up by Sutton, but then the rest of the night porbably didn't go as he had expected.

Armed with several knives and an axe, she cut his legs and drank his blood straight from the open wounds. She stabbed him in his chest several times, and McDaniel, fearing for his life, tried to get loose. The escape attempt succeeded, and Sutton was sentenced to 10 years in prison for the incident.

Bertrand, Kürten, Haigh, Wigginton, Chase, Sellers, Semenuha and Sutton are all exampled of murderers who have been called 'vampires' in the aftermath of their actions. The next section will be a selection of deeds carried out by individuals who called themselves – Vampires.

James Riva (1957- , USA)

James Riva developed an interest in blood when he was five years old and at the age of 13 he began to kill smaller animals. When he was 17 years old, he told his therapist that he planned to kill his father. This, of course, frightened the parents, who reacted by installing a lock in their bedroom door. They also started sleeping in shifts.

James suffered from delusions. He heard voices speaking to him and was convinced that his parents, and even his grandmother, were in fact vampires.

After a few weeks, his mother asked a court to move James from the home as the situation was unbearable. James then moved to his own apartment, but a few months later he called his parents and told them that people were out to kill him. He told them that he met vampires who gave him blood, but he wanted to get out of that crowd. He then moved back home. Shortly after, his mother found feces, blood and animal parts in his room.

James moved out yet again but received complaints from the landlord when his room was full of engravings made with a knife. The landlord also found a dead cat in the wardrobe, which had been decapitated with the brain removed from the skull.

James claimed that he did it to examine the brain so that he could figure out what was wrong with his own. He had also drunk the blood of the cat.

He thought that the only thing that would help was to become a vampire, which he would become by committing murder and drinking human blood. James suspected that the grandmother, who was in a wheelchair, poisoned the food and drank his blood at night.

In 1980, when James was 22 years old, he murdered his grandmother. The grandmother was shot to death with bullets painted with gold paint. James supposedly then proceeded to drink blood from the bullet holes. The murder ended with him lighting the body on fire afterwards.

When he was arrested for the murder, he said that the grandmother's blood was too old, so the deed did not make him the immortal vampire he craved to be. In his testimony after the murder, James also stated that he knew he was sick and that he heard voices, something he had done for a long time. The voices mocked him and said he was a bad person who had not killed anyone. On the day of the murder, the voices told him that he would die if he did not kill the grandmother.

James himself has said that he previously drank blood over the period of a decade. His theory is that when one drinks human blood, the body gets used to it and if the consumption stops, the body begins to consume its own muscle tissue which leads to weight loss. There is reason to be skeptical about his reasoning because weight loss cannot be linked to blood consumption for physiological reasons. James believes that drinking blood is very addictive, and he had withdrawal symptoms when he quit.

There seem to be several uncertainties about James's perception of reality and thus his motive for the murder. He longed to become a vampire himself, while fearing them at the same time. James killed the grandmother because he thought she was a vampire who stole his blood, while saying he himself would become a vampire if he took her life. During the investigation of the murder, when James was questioned, he actually stated that he had been a vampire for several years. He claimed that he had socialized with other vampires, and that voices instructed him to kill. His reward for the murders, according to James himself, was the opportunity for eternal life.

James Riva was convicted for murder and received lifetime imprisonment.

Allan Menzies (1981 - 2004, Scotland)

Allan Menzies was obsessed with the movie *The Queen of the Damned,* which is based on Anne Rice's book of the same name. He had seen the film hundreds of times, sometimes several times a same day. Ironically, it was his later victim Thomas McKendrick who had loaned him the movie. He believed that he and the main character of the movie, the vampire Akasha, had an agreement where he would have eternal life if he provided her need with souls.

On December 11, 2002, Allan visited his friend Thomas. They began to discuss vampirism and Thomas questioned Allan's belief in vampires. The confrontation made Allan upset, and armed with a knife and a hammer, he attacked his friend. After the murder, he drank his friend's blood and also ate parts of his head. After the feast, he dug a grave and buried the body.

Five weeks after the murder, the police found the buried body and the evidence pointed to Allan. He was sentenced to life in prison and was classified as a psychopath. He claimed that he had been ordered to kill the friend by 'The Queen of the Damned', Akasha, and that he would become immortal in the next life.

After a year in prison, Allan Menzie's was found dead in his cell. The cause of death was assumed to be suicide.

Manuela Ruda (1978- , Germany) and Daniel Ruda (1975- , Germany)

Both Manuela and Daniel Ruda were interested in satanism and they shared a dark view of life.

Manuela had come into contact with satanism at the age of 16 when she left home in 1995. She was interested in extreme ways of living and had contacted the so-called 'leopard man', Tom Leppard, who lived in Scotland. Leppard agreed to let Manuela live with him and she moved in. It was during that period that she also came into contact with vampirists and she has said that she participated in various blood ceremonies in England. After a few years abroad, Manuela returned to Germany, and she had also acquired permanent fangs. How it all really happened is up for debate. Some say she herself grinded her own teeth, while others claim she installed real teeth from a predator.

The year was now 1999 and elsewhere in Germany Daniel Ruda sent in a personal ad to one of the country's music magazines. Daniel claimed in the advertisement to be a 'vampire' who sought a 'princess of darkness who hates everything and everyone'. Manuela saw the ad and decided to answer it. The couple started a relationship and shortly thereafter they moved in together.

Together, they cultivated their common fascination for satanism and vampirism, including traveling to Scotland and England to take part in the subcultures there. It can only be speculated what happened during their joint excursions as their increasingly morbid thoughts were born. They were both convinced that they had sold their souls to Satan and the devil demanded blood sacrifices. Initially it was goats and chickens, but it would soon get worse.

The couple married in June 2001 and one month later, they invited Frank Haagen, one of Daniel's colleagues over. The unsuspecting colleague was stabbed 66 times and then had a pentagram carved into his chest, after which the couple worshiped Satan together.

During the rite they both drank of the victim's blood from a bowl on an altar made of skulls. The deed was then celebrated by the couple having intercourse in a coffin next to the body. Normally, the coffin was the sleeping place for Manuela.

After having sex, Manuela and Daniel drove off in their car to await Satan's next order. With them in the car they had a chainsaw. It is unknown if Satan gave them any new orders, because the couple was arrested shortly after at a gas station.

When the body was found, there was still a scalpel left in the body, which protruded from the victim's stomach. A death list with names of potential future victims was also found.

They both confessed to the murder, but they did not take any responsibility because they were both Satan's instruments and only followed instructions. Manula and Daniel Ruda were sentenced to 13 and 15 years of psychiatric care

Rod Ferrell (1980- , USA)

At an early age, Rod Ferrell was sexually assaulted by a close relative and had a generally horrific upbringing. The father abandoned him when he was a child and he grew up with his dysfunctional mother.

He was something of an outsider in the town he grew up in, bu the was very much involved with his girlfriend Heather Wendorf. None of them had especially many friends and they had a common interest in vampires and the occult. They were separated from each other when Rod moved with his mother to another city, but they kept in touch via telephone. Heather often talked about her overly protective parents and together they made plans to run away together. In some telephone conversations, she also mentioned that she wished her parents dead, something that Rod probably read into more seriously than she meant it to be.

Rod was a charismatic person and discovered early that he had a natural ability to captivate his audience. After moving, he benefited from his ability and he soon had en entourage of other alienated young people. The group played the roleplaying game *Vampire: The Masquerade* and they also formed their own vampirist group where they performed various rituals together. Within the group, called the *Kentucky Vampire Clan* (KVC), they sacrificed animals to Satan, drank each other's blood, and Rod sometimes cut himself in public because he liked the attention it created.

Rod was the natural leader and soon began to claim that he was a 500-year-old true vampire and incarnation of Satan himself. The vampirist group was subsequently defined as a sect and suspected of having had around 35 members.

Two months before the murders, the police began to keep their eyes on the group because Rod had been convicted of animal cruelty. He broke into a dog shelter and injureed over 50 severely, of which a total of three died. A dog ha dits legs severed, which were never found.

In 1996, when Rod was 16 years old, his mother was accused of premeditated rape and sodomy. The mother had written a letter filled with sexual content to a 14-year-old boy at it was discovered when his parents found the letters. The letters also revealed that the mother wanted to become a 'vampire' and wanted the boy to transform her. The police investigation showed that she had an emotional maturity equivalent to a 12-year-old. She dressed in gothic clothing and expressed a wish to be part of her son's vampirist group. The mother was later tried and convicted for the premeditated crimes.

A few days after the accusations against his mother became known, Rod decided to drive all the way to his girlfriend Heather. He brought along his friends Dana

Cooper, Charity Lynn Keesee and Howard Scott Anderson, and judging by the fully packed car, an escape was planned. Twelve hours later, they arrived at Heather's house, and Heather boarded the car.

Before they continued the journey, Rod excused himself and entered Heathers parent's house- According to some sources, Howard followed Rod into the house. Inside the house, Heather's father, Richard, lay on the couch and slept, her mother Naoma stood in the shower. Richard was killed first with a crowbar and Naoma was then stabbed in the head. Both victims' skulls were crushed, indicating a brutal assault. Rod then used a cigarette to burn a 'V' on Richard's chest – a signature for the KVC.

Meanwhile, the others drove to a nearby cemetery to conduct an initiation ceremony with Heather, with the purpose of making her a member of the vampirist group. When Rod reunited with the rest of the group in the car, he told them that he had murdered Heather's parents, which his friends and girlfriend misinterpreted as a joke. Together, the group continued their journey to New Orleans.

On December 5, 1996, the British news magazine The Independent reported that is was Heather's sister who discovered the bodies and subsequently called the police. Suspicions were directed quickly to the group.

The police found them through one of the women, Charity, who contacted her parents and telling them where they were because the group had started to run out of food and monet. Charity agreed with her mother to meet up at a hotel. The mother forwarded the information to the police and the subsequent arrest was made.

Rod himself did not think that he could get arrested because he was a 'real vampire' and therefore above the law and its representatives. Initially, Rod denied the allegations and instead accused another vampirist clan of the deed. Rod also claimed that he had been diagnosed with multiple personality disorder and that he was a member of a satanic sect ruled by his grandfather. In 1998, the trial began, and Rod confessed to his crime.

Of all KVC members, only Rod has still recently claimed that he is a vampire. Scott received a life sentence while both Dana and Charity have served their time at the time of the writing. Heather was released when it was deemed likely that she did not know anything about the murders.

Rod Ferrell first received the death penalty for murder, which made him the youngest person ever to receive a death sentence in Florida's history. Later, the sentence was changed into life imprisonment.

Lennart Persson (date of birth unknown, Sweden)

Lennart Persson, also known as 'The Swedish Cannibal', was the first confirmed case of criminal vampirism in Sweden. In an interview with the Swedish newspaper *Aftonbladet* in April 27, 2009, Lennart claimed that he is both a vampire and cannibal and thus has a thirst for blood. He now serves his sentence in the form of psychiatric care after a double murder in 2005, where he, among other things, drank his victims' blood.

Joshua Rudiger (1976-, USA)

Joshua Rudiger grew up in several foster families and psychiatric institutions. At the age of four, he was diagnosed as psychotic. When he turned 18, he was released from an institution, and soon after began to walk a more violent path. In 1997 he injured a friend with a bow and was then diagnosed with schizophrenia and bipolar disorder.

A year after, in 1998, he began to kill. He cut the throats of homeless people in his hometown of San

Francisco. Three men were injured, and one woman died.

It was the same year, at the age of 22, that he was arrested. Joshua then claimed that, in fact, he was a 2000-year-old vampire and that he was in need of human blood. He had a history of mental health issues and had earlier claimed that he was a ninja warrior.

Joshua was sentenced to 23 years in prison for his deeds.

Matthew Hardman (1984- , England)

Matthew Hardman was interested in vampires, especially to their immortality. He owned a large collection of books on the subject and was a regular visitor to various vampire-related websites. His fascination grew so strong that he believed that vampires existed and that they could give him eternal life.

On November 22, 2001, his conviction prompted him to stab a 90-year-old woman 22 times. He opened up her chest and removed her heart. The heart was later found in a frying pan with lip imprints on it. Matthew also cut open the woman's legs and drank her blood. Het hen places candles and a crucifix-like object by the body. In 2002, he was sentenced to life imprisonment for the murder.

Epilogue

THEN WHAT IS IT that makes a person believe to be one, or wish to be, a vampire? Possibly it has to do with the image of the vampire as attractive, successful and exciting. It can also be about group affiliation, and that could be why some people are seeking out vampire culture.

It also gives personal power, something that may stem from lack of it earlier in life. It becomes a way to feel special, chosen and powerful. It can also generate a lot of attention – something people naturally seek, because we all want to feel recognized, or accepted, in one way or another.

For those who want to dive deeper into the world of real vampires, my advice is to go through the reference list. There is a lot of exciting literature on the subject, primarily in English. The Internet is also an effective tool when looking for information. If you are lucky enough to have access to a scientific database, you should enter some vampire related keywords and see what you can find.

This book has primarily focused on giving insight into the vampire subculture. My purpose has not been to judge or to present a 'true' picture, so I have deliberately not written much criticism. I am not interested in arguing against the existence of the vampire. My interest has, instead, always been to learn more about the exciting subculture that is vampirism – regardless of whether the beliefs of other people correspond to reality or not. A simple search on the internet shows websites that are dedicated to proving that vampires do not exist. Whatever your believes are, I hope you've found the book entertaining and interesting.

So, what do I think? I am a skeptic and non-believer. My personal assessment is that there is no research showing that vampires exist. However, it is impossible to deny that there are people among us who believe themselves to be vampires. For some, this may be a way to find an identity, while for others it is a part of extensive mental health issues. The majority of the self-identified vampirists do not suffer from their condition. Instead, vampirism is something that makes them feel good. As long as their well-being does not hurt other people, I see no need to criticize their way of life.

Cecilia Fredriksson

From the Author

I hope you liked my book about real vampires. I am currently working on a few projects – this time, though, it's fiction. If you want to make sure that you're always updated about my newest releases, current giveaways, sneak peaks, free books and special offers, all you have to do is sign up for my newsletter. You find it on this website:

https://mailchi.mp/e2f264b0d2d5/vampirist

It is also possible to opt-in on my homepage: www.ceciliafredriksson.net

Best regards,
Cecilia Fredriksson

About the Author

Cecilia Fredriksson (born 1987 in Eskilstuna, Sverige) is an educated social worker. She debuted in 2018 with the book *Vampirist: A Book About Real Vampires*.

Facebook:
https://www.facebook.com/makaberbooks/
Instagram: @makaber_books
Twitter: @CeciliaMakaber
Homepage: www.ceciliafredriksson.net
E-mail address: info@ceciliafredriksson.net

References

Chapter 1

Apergis, N. (2016). Makaber vampyrgrav funnen i Polen. *Världens historia*, 14th December. http://varldenshistoria.se/samhalle/mytologi/makab er-vampyrgravfunnen-i-polen

Beresford, M. (2014). *'For the Blood is the Life': Blood, Disease and the Vampire Myth in the Early Modern Period.* The Blood Project Conference, St Anne´s College, Oxford, 10th January 2014.

Bundasen, L. (1998). *The Natural History of Vampires.* Lehigh Review, 6:2, 5-16.

Burridge, T. (2004). *Reply to a Vampire.* Psychodynamic Practice: Individuals, Groups and Organisations, 10:2, 255-268. DOI: 10.1080/14753630410001716038.

Cox, A. M. (1995). *Porphyria and Vampirism: Another Myth In the Making.* Post-graduate Medicine Journal, 71, 643-644.

Dalén, K. (2014).'Vampyrgrav' funnen i Bulgarien. *Dagens Nyheter,* 14th October. https://www.dn.se/nyheter/varlden/vampyrgrav-funnen-i-bulgarien/

Ericson, E. & Ericson, T. (2008). *Illustrerade medicinska sjukdomar: specifik omvårdnad, medicinsk behandling, patofysiologi.* Third edition. Lund: Studentlitteratur AB.

Harrison Lindbergh, K. (2010). *Vampyrernas Historia.* Stockholm: Norstedts.

Hampl, J.S., Hampl, W.S. (1997). *Pellagra and the origin of a myth: evidence from European literature and folklore.* J R Soc Med, 1997;90, 636-639.

Illis, L. (1964). *On Porphyria and the Etiology of Werewolves.* Section of the History of Medicine, vol 57 January, 23-26.

Jackson, K. (2009). *Bite: A Vampire Handbook.* London: Portobello Books Ltd.

Kaliff, A. (2009). *Dracula och han arv: myt, fakta, fiktion.* Nacka: Bokförlaget Efron & Dotter AB.

Kayton, L. (1972). *The Relationship of the Vampire Legend to Schizofrenia.* Journal of Youth and Adolescent, vol 1, nr 4, 303-314.

Kvarnkullen, T. (2014). Här är fynden som kan lösa vampyrgåtan. *Expressen,* 27th November. https://www.expressen.se/nyheter/inloggad/har-ar-fynden-som-kanlosa-vampyrgatan/

Laycock, J. (2009). *Vampires Today: The Truth About Modern Vampirism.* Westport: Praeger Publishers.

Maas, R.P.PW.M. & Voets, P.J.G.M. (2014). *The Vampire in medical perspective: myth or malady?*. Q J Med, 107, 945-946. DOI: 10.1093/qjmed/hcu159

Page, C. (1991). *Bloodlust: conversations with real vampires*. New York: HarperCollins Publishers.

Santos, L.C., Lucinda, L.R., Santos, A.C. & Silva, L.D. (2011). *Medical Explanations for the Myth of Vampirism*. DOI: 10.5935/2238-3182.20130080

Summers, M. (2009). *The Vampire his kith and kin: the real twilight world of the vampire within society*. CreateSpace Independent Publishing Platform.

Tiziani, M. (2009). *Vampires and Vampirism: Pathological Roots of a Myth*. Antrocom, 5:2, 133-137.

Belanger, M. (Red.) (2007). *Vampires in their own words: An Anthology of Vampire Voices.* Woodbury Minnesota: Llewellyn Publications.

Byttner, K.-J. (2017). Forskaren som knäckt koden för att bli 1000 år gammal – hans metod ska försena åldrandet och stoppa livshotande sjukdomar. *Veckans affärer,* 23th February. https://www.va.se/nyheter/2017/02/23/forskaren-somknackt-koden-for-att-bli-1000-ar-gammal--hans-metod-ska-forsena-aldrandetoch-stoppa-livshotande-sjukdomar/

DiSaturni, A. (1998). *The Order of the Vampyre of The Temple of Set – A Scholarly Study.*

Hemphill, R. E. & Zabov, T. (1983). *Clinical Vampirism: a presentation of 3 cases and re-evaluation of Haigh, the 'acid-bath murderer'.* Sa Medical Journal, vol 63, 19th February 1983. 278-281.

Izidari. (2011a). *The Truth: Real Vampires.* Blurb.

Izidari. (2011b). *Real Vampires.* Blurb.

Kayton, L. (1972). *The Relationship of the Vampire Legend to Schizofrenia.* Journal of Youth and Adolescent, vol 1, nr 4, 303-314.

Keyworth, D. (2002). *The Socio-Religious Beliefs and Nature of the Contemporary Vampire Subculture.* Journal of Contemporary Religion, vol 17, no 3, 355-370.

Laycock, J. (2009). *Vampires Today: The Truth About Modern Vampirism.* Westport: Praeger Publishers.

Meyer, S. (2006). *Om jag kunde drömma.* Stockholm: B. Wahlströms förlag.

Page, C. (1991). *Bloodlust: conversations with real vampires.* New York: HarperCollins Publishers.

Ramsland, K. (1998). *Piercing the Darkness: Undercover with Vampires in America Today.* Oxford: Boxtree.

Ramsland, K. (2002). *The Science of Vampires.* New York: The Berkley Publishing Group.

Russo, A. (2008). *Vampire Nation.* Woodbury Minnesota: Llewellyn Publications.

Ward, B. (2003). *Läkekonstens historia: läkekonst från hela världen och genom tidsåldrarna.* Stockholm: Valentin Förlag AB.

Williams, E., Robbins, M. & Picton, L. (2006). *Adolescent television viewing and belief in Vampires.* Journal of Beliefs & Values: Studies in Religion and Education, 27:2, 227-229. DOI: 10.1080/13617670600850000

Andersen, H. & Kaspersen, L. B. (Red.) (2007). *Klassisk och modern samhällsteori*. Lund: Studentlitteratur AB.

Gubb, K., Segal, J., Khota, A. & Dicks, A. (2006). *Clinical Vampirism: a review and illustrative case report*. S Afr PsychiAtry Rev 2006.9 163-168.

Hemphill, R. E. & Zabov, T. (1983). *Clinical Vampirism: a presentation of 3 cases and re-evaluation of Haigh, the 'acid-bath murderer'*. Sa Medical Journal, vol 63, 19th February 1983. 278-281.

Jaffé, P. D. & DiCataldo, F. (1994). *Clinical Vampirism: Blending Myth and Reality*. The Bulletin of the American Academy of Psychiatry and the Law, vol 22, no 4, 533-544.

Keyworth, D. (2002). *The Socio-Religious Beliefs and Nature of the Contemporary Vampire Subculture*. Journal of Contemporary Religion, vol 17, no 3, 355-370.

Krafft-Ebing, R. (2011). *Psychopathia Sexualis: The Classic Study of Deviant Sex*. New York: Arcade Publishing.

Noll, R. (1990). *Bizarre Diseases of the Mind*. New York: Berkley Books.

Noll, R. (2007). *The Encyclopedia of Schizophrenia and Other Psychotic Disorders*, third edition. New York: Facts On File, Inc.

Olry, R. & Haines, D.E. (2011). *Renfield's Syndrome: A Psychiatric Illness Drawn from Bram Stoker's Dracula*. Journal of the History of the Neurosciences: Basic and Clinical Perspectives, 20:4, 368-371. DOI: 10.1080/0964704X.2011.595655

Prins, H. (1984). *Vampirism - Legendary of Clinical Phenomenon?*. Med Sci Law 24:4, 283-293.

Prins, H. (1985). *Vampirism: A Clinical Condition*. British Journal of Psychiatry, 146, 666-668.

Tiziani, M. (2009). *Vampires and Vampirism: Pathological Roots of a Myth*. Antrocom, 5:2, 133.137.

Belanger, M. (Red.) (2007). *Vampires in their own words: An Anthology of Vampire Voices.* Woodbury Minnesota: Llewellyn Publications.

Cohen, D. (1995). *Real Vampires.* New York: Coddlehill Books.

Dresser, N. (1989). *American Vampires: fans, victims, practitioners.* New York: Vintage Books.

Guiley, R. E. (1991). *Vampires among us.* New York: Pocket Books.

Izidari. (2011b). *Real Vampires.* Blurb.

Keyworth, D. (2002). *The Socio-Religious Beliefs and Nature of the Contemporary Vampire Subculture.* Journal of Contemporary Religion, vol 17, no 3, 355-370.

Laycock, J. (2009). *Vampires Today: The Truth About Modern Vampirism.* Westport: Praeger Publishers.

Queens Vampire Research Center. (2012). http://qvrc.blogspot.se/

Ramsland, K. (1998). *Piercing the Darkness: Undercover with Vampires in America Today*. Oxford: Boxtree.

Real Vampires Support Page. (1999). http://sphynxcatvp.nocturna.org/

Russo, A. (2005). *The Real Twilight*. London: John Blake Publishing Ltd.

Russo, A. (2008). *Vampire Nation*. Woodbury Minnesota: Llewellyn Publications.

Sanguinarius. (1997). http://www.sanguinarius.org/

Vampires Are Not Real. (n.d.). http://realvamps.weebly.com/real-vampires.html

Williams, DJ. (2008). *Contemporary Vampires and (Blood-Red) Leisure: Should We Be Afraid of the Dark?*. Ontario Research Council on Leisure, 32(2), 513-539.

Williams, DJ. (2013). *Social Work, BDSM and Vampires: Toward Understanding and Empowering People with Non-traditional Identities*. Canadian Social Work, Vol 15 Nr 1, 10-24.

Belanger, M. (Red.) (2007). *Vampires in their own words: An Anthology of Vampire Voices.* Woodbury Minnesota: Llewellyn Publications.

Guiley, R. E. (1991). *Vampires among us.* New York: Pocket Books.

Hyman, R. (1999). *Vampire of the body: The politics of chronic fatigue syndrome.* Woman & Performance: a journal of feminist theory, 11:1, 187-201, DOI: 10.1080/07407709908571322.

Izidari. (2011a). *The Truth: Real Vampires.* Blurb.

Izidari. (2011b). *Real Vampires.* Blurb.

Keyworth, D. (2002). *The Socio-Religious Beliefs and Nature of the Contemporary Vampire Subculture.* Journal of Contemporary Religion, vol 17, no 3, 355-370.

Russo, A. (2005). *The Real Twilight.* London: John Blake Publishing Ltd.

Russo, A. (2008). *Vampire Nation*. Woodbury
Minnesota: Llewellyn Publications.

Belanger, M. (Red.) (2007). *Vampires in their own words: An Anthology of Vampire Voices*. Woodbury Minnesota: Llewellyn Publications.

Dahlqvist, A. (2016). *Bara lite blod: ett reportage om mens och makt*. Stockholm: Bokförlaget Atlas.

Dresser, N. (1989). *American Vampires: fans, victims, practitioners*. New York: Vintage Books.

Guiley, R. E. (1991). *Vampires among us*. New York: Pocket Books.

Halevy, A., Levi, Y., Shnaker, A. & Orda, R. (1989). *Auto-vampirism: an unusual cause of anaemia*. Journal of the Royal Society of Medicine, vol 82. Oktober 1989, 630-631.

Izidari. (2011a). *The Truth: Real Vampires*. Blurb.

Jaffé, P. D. & DiCataldo, F. (1994). *Clinical Vampirism: Blending Myth and Reality*. The Bulletin of the American Academy of Psychiatry and the Law, vol 22, no 4, 533-544.

Karlsson, A-M., Hald, F. (1994). *Kapa ben och tappa blod - historien om konsten att bota*. Stockholm: Rabén & Sjögren.

Keyworth, D. (2002). *The Socio-Religious Beliefs and Nature of the Contemporary Vampire Subculture*. Journal of Contemporary Religion, vol 17, no 3, 355-370.

Laycock, J. (2009). *Vampires Today: The Truth About Modern Vampirism*. Westport: Praeger Publishers.

Leighton, S. (2005b). *How to know if you are a real vampire.*
http://www.vampirewebsite.net/howknowifavampire.html

Leighton, S. (2005e). *Getting blood made easy.*
http://vampirewebsite.net/gettingblood.html

Noll, R. (1990). *Bizarre Diseases of the Mind*. New York: Berkley Books.

Page, C. (1991). *Bloodlust: conversations with real vampires*. New York: HarperCollins Publishers.

Prins, H. (1985). *Vampirism: A Clinical Condition.* British Journal of Psychiatry, 146, 666-668.

Ramsland, K. (2002). *The Science of Vampires.* New York: The Berkley Publishing Group.

Russo, A. (2005). *The Real Twilight.* London: John Blake Publishing Ltd.

Russo, A. (2008). *Vampire Nation.* Woodbury Minnesota: Llewellyn Publications.

Tiziani, M. (2009). *Vampires and Vampirism: Pathological Roots of a Myth.* Antrocom, 5:2, 133-137.

Vampire Donor Database. (2015). http://www.shadowlore.net/VampireDonorDatabase .html

Ward, B. (2003). *Läkekonstens historia: läkekonst från hela världen och genom tidsåldrarna.* Stockholm: Valentin Förlag AB.

Williams, DJ. (2008). *Contemporary Vampires and (Blood-Red) Leisure: Should We Be Afraid of the Dark?*. Ontario Research Council on Leisure, 32(2), 513-539.

Williams, DJ. (2013). *Social Work, BDSM and Vampires: Toward Understanding and Empowering People with Non-traditional Identities*. Canadian Social Work, Vol 15 Nr 1, 10-24.

Belanger, M. (Red.) (2007). *Vampires in their own words: An Anthology of Vampire Voices*. Woodbury Minnesota: Llewellyn Publications.

Brander, R. & Lehtilä, B. (2005). *Vampyr*. Stockholm: Bonnier Carlsen.

Gubb, K., Segal, J., Khota, A. & Dicks, A. (2006). *Clinical Vampirism: a review and illustrative case report*. S Afr PsychiAtry Rev 2006.9 163-168.

Izidari. (2011a). *The Truth: Real Vampires*. Blurb.

Keyworth, D. (2002). *The Socio-Religious Beliefs and Nature of the Contemporary Vampire Subculture*. Journal of Contemporary Religion, vol 17, no 3, 355-370.

Laycock, J. (2009). *Vampires Today: The Truth About Modern Vampirism*. Westport: Praeger Publishers.

Leighton, S. (2005f). *This is the truth about energy vampires*.
http://www.vampirewebsite.net/energyvampires.html

Melton, G. J. Phd. (1994). *The Vampire Book: The Encyclopedia of the Undead*. Visible Ink Press.

Ramsland, K. (1998). *Piercing the Darkness: Undercover with Vampires in America Today*. Oxford: Boxtree.

Russo, A. (2005). *The Real Twilight*. London: John Blake Publishing Ltd.

Russo, A. (2008). *Vampire Nation*. Woodbury Minnesota: Llewellyn Publications.

Stanwey, A. (1997). *Stora naturläkarboken: Hälsa och naturmedicin för hela familjen*. Västerås: ICA-förlaget AB.

Wilson, N. (2000). *A Psychoanalytic Contribution to Psychic Vampirism: A Case Vignette*. The American Journal of Psychoanalysis, vol 60, no 2, 177-186.

Williams, DJ. (2008). *Contemporary Vampires and (Blood-Red) Leisure: Should We Be Afraid of the Dark?*. Ontario Research Council on Leisure, 32(2), 513-539.

Belanger, M. (Red.) (2007). *Vampires in their own words: An Anthology of Vampire Voices*. Woodbury Minnesota: Llewellyn Publications.

DiSaturni, A. (n.d.). *An Overview of the Definitions of a Vampire and on Contemporary Vampirism*. https://groups.yahoo.com/neo/groups/vampire-gangrel/conversations/topics/20

DiSaturni, A. (1998). *The Order of the Vampyre of The Temple of Set – A Scholarly Study*.

Dresser, N. (1989). *American Vampires: fans, victims, practitioners*. New York: Vintage Books.

Harrison Lindbergh, K. (2010). *Vampyrernas Historia*. Stockholm: Norstedts.

Keyworth, D. (2002). *The Socio-Religious Beliefs and Nature of the Contemporary Vampire Subculture*. Journal of Contemporary Religion, vol 17, no 3, 355-370.

LaVey, A. S. (1976). *The Satanic Bible*. New York: Avon Books.

Laycock, J. (2009). *Vampires Today: The Truth About Modern Vampirism*. Westport: Praeger Publishers. Miller, T.W., Veltkamp, L.J., Kraus, R.F.,

Lane, T. & Heister, T. (1999). *An Adolescent Vampire Cult in Rural America: Clinical Issues and Case Study*. Child Psychiatry and Human Development, vol 29(3), spring 1999, 209-219.

Ordo Sekhemu. (2000). http://www.ordosekhemu.org

Partridge, C. (Red.) (2004). *Nya religioner: en uppslagsbok om andliga rörelser, sekter och alternativ andlighet*. Örebro: Bokförlaget Libris.

Ramsland, K. (1998). *Piercing the Darkness: Undercover with Vampires in America Today*. Oxford: Boxtree.

Russo, A. (2005). *The Real Twilight*. London: John Blake Publishing Ltd.

Russo, A. (2008). *Vampire Nation*. Woodbury Minnesota: Llewellyn Publications.

Svahn, C. (2012). *Sekter, hemliga sällskap och domedagsprofeter*. Sundbyberg: Bokförlaget Semic.

The Temple of the Vampire. (n.d.).
http://templeofthevampire.com/

Aftonbladet. (27th April 2009). *Jag känner blodtörsten varje dag.* By P. Tagesson.
http://www.aftonbladet.se/nyheter/article11787266.ab

Biondi, R. & Hecox, W. (1992). *The Dracula Killer.* London: Mondo.

Bundasen, L. (1998). *The Natural History of Vampires.* Lehigh Review, 6:2, 5-16.

Edwards, W. (2013). *The Lonely Hearts Vampire: The Bizarre and Horrifying True Account of Serial Killer Bela Kiss.* Absolute Crime Books.

Faye, A. (2013). *Serial Killers.* E-bok. ISBN: 9781304315168

Harrison Lindbergh, K. (2010). *Vampyrernas Historia.* Stockholm: Norstedts.

Izidari. (2011a). *The Truth: Real Vampires.* Blurb.

Jaffé, P. D. & DiCataldo, F. (1994). *Clinical Vampirism: Blending Myth and Reality*. The Bulletin of the American Academy of Psychiatry and the Law, vol 22, no 4, 533-544.

Kayton, L. (1972). *The Relationship of the Vampire Legend to Schizofrenia*. Journal of Youth and Adolescent, vol 1, nr 4, 303-314.

Keyworth, D. (2002). *The Socio-Religious Beliefs and Nature of the Contemporary Vampire Subculture*. Journal of Contemporary Religion, vol 17, no 3, 355-370.

LaVey, A. S. (1976). *The Satanic Bible*. New York: Avon Books.

Laycock, J. (2009). *Vampires Today: The Truth About Modern Vampirism*. Westport: Praeger Publishers.

Linedecker, C. L. (1998). *The Vampire Killers: A Horrifying True Story of Bloodshed and Murder*. New York: St. Martin's Press.

Miller, T.W., Veltkamp, L.J., Kraus, R.F., Lane, T. &
Heister, T. (1999). *An Adolescent Vampire Cult in Rural
America: Clinical Issues and Case Study*. Child
Psychiatry and Human Development, vol 29(3),
spring 1999, 209-219.

Monaco, R. & Burt, W. (1993). *The Dracula Syndrome*.
London: Headline Book Publishing.

Noll, R. (1990). *Bizarre Diseases of the Mind*. New
York: Berkley Books.

Olry, R. & Haines, D.E. (2011). *Renfield's Syndrome: A
Psychiatric Illness Drawn from Bram Stoker's Dracula*.
Journal of the History of the Neurosciences: Basic
and Clinical Perspectives, 20:4, 368-371. DOI:
10.1080/0964704X.2011.595655

Page, C. (1991). *Bloodlust: conversations with real
vampires*. New York: HarperCollins Publishers.

Picart, C.J.S. (2006). *Crime and the Gothic: Sexualizing
Serial Killers*. Journal of Criminal Justice and Popular
Culture, 13(1), 1-18.

Prins, H. (1985). *Vampirism: A Clinical Condition.* British Journal of Psychiatry, 146, 666-668.

Prins, H. (1990). *Bizarre Behaviours: Boundaries of Psychiatric Disorder.* London: Routledge.

Ramsland, K. (n.d.). *Vampire Killers: Renfield's Syndrome.* http://www.crimelibrary.com/serial_killers/weird/vampires/7.html

Ramsland, K. (1998). *Piercing the Darkness: Undercover with Vampires in America Today.* Oxford: Boxtree.

Ramsland, K. (2002). *The Science of Vampires.* New York: The Berkley Publishing Group.

Russo, A. (2005). *The Real Twilight.* London: John Blake Publishing Ltd.

Russo, A. (2008). *Vampire Nation.* Woodbury Minnesota: Llewellyn Publications.

The Independent. (5th December 1996). "Blood ties". By D. Jeffreys. http://www.independent.co.uk/life-style/blood-ties-1313032.html

Weston, T. (2010). *Britain's Bloodiest Serial Killers: From the Vampire Killer to the Crossbow Cannibal*. Swordworks Books.

Williams, DJ. (2008). *Contemporary Vampires and (Blood-Red) Leisure: Should We Be Afraid of the Dark?*. Ontario Research Council on Leisure, 32(2), 513-539.

Williams, DJ. (2013). *Social Work, BDSM and Vampires: Toward Understanding and Empowering People with Non-traditional Identities*. Canadian Social Work, Vol 15 Nr 1, 10-24.

9 789177 734482